A Country Recipe Notebook

by the same author

COOKING FOR CHRISTMAS

COTTAGE AND COUNTRY RECIPES

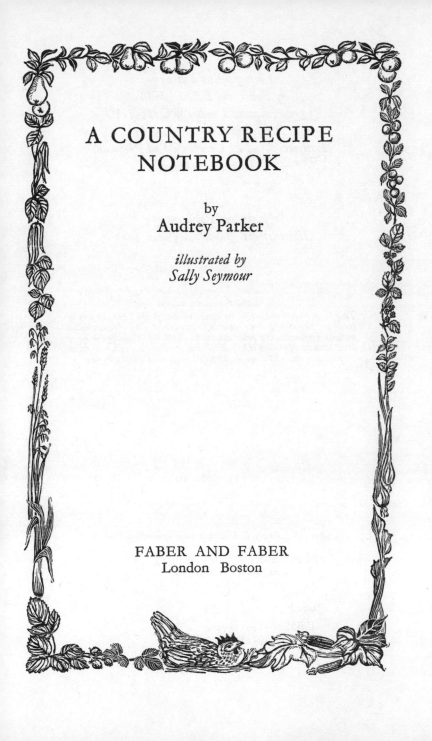

A COUNTRY RECIPE NOTEBOOK

by
Audrey Parker

illustrated by
Sally Seymour

FABER AND FABER
London Boston

First published in 1979
by Faber and Faber Limited
3 Queen Square London WC1N 3AU
Printed in Great Britain by
Latimer Trend & Company Ltd Plymouth
All rights reserved

British Library Cataloguing in Publication Data

Parker, Audrey
    A country recipe notebook.
    1. Cookery, English
    I. Title
    641.5'942   TX717

    ISBN 0-571-11392-3
    ISBN 0-571-11417-2 Pbk

Contents

Acknowledgements

I am very grateful to all those who have given me permission to quote from copyright sources:

Garnstone Press/Geoffrey Bles, *The Shining Levels* by John Wyatt; Farmers Weekly, *Farmhouse Fare* (country recipes collected by Farmers Weekly); W. Foulsham & Co. Ltd. who own the copyright, *Old English Cookery* by Peggy Hutchinson; The Authors' Literary Estates and Chatto and Windus Ltd., *The Gentle Art of Cookery* by Mrs. C. F. Leyel and Miss Olga Hartley; Oxford University Press, *Lark Rise to Candleford* by Flora Thompson (World's Classics edition 1954).

Introduction

This book is mainly for incidentals, including background, hints, customs, words and phrases, materials, methods, ways of adapting and ways in which ideas from the past tie up with modern research.

Some of the recipes mentioned are given in my book on *Cottage and Country Recipes*, a collection designed to fit in with the needs of today. The two books are quite separate, but when we collect country recipes we usually need to collect many extra details as well, and these notes are for filling in some of the gaps.

Notes on Using the Recipes

The recipes included are in the simplest country traditions. This is a difficult but an important time to be writing about traditional recipes. It would be a great pity if people came to feel they could not use an old recipe unless it had already been converted to metric measures. Many valuable links with the past would be lost. For this reason I am keeping to the imperial measures and including keys for conversion (as nearly as practicable) to metric. In any case most country cookery in the past was done without benefit of scales, and the right quantities (which may not be quite the same from one person's view to another's) are usually easily judged, especially with practice.

Many country recipes are simply measured by cupfuls, which nowadays some people prefer to avoid. When using the older recipes it is useful to remember that a 'cup', unless otherwise indicated, is usually reckoned as containing 8 fluid oz (about 225 ml); a 'breakfastcup', ½ pint or 10 fluid oz (about 300 ml); and a 'teacup', ¼ pint (1 gill) or 5 fluid oz (about 150 ml).

GUIDE TO METRIC WEIGHTS AND MEASURES

Exact Equivalents

1 oz = 28·35 grams   1 pint = 0·568 litre

Working Equivalents

½ oz = 15 grams   ¼ pint = 150 millilitres
1 oz = 25 grams   ½ pint = 300 millilitres
2 oz = 50 grams   ¾ pint = 450 millilitres
4 oz = 125 grams   1 pint = 550/600 millilitres
6 oz = 175 grams   1¾ pints = 1 litre
8 oz = 225 grams   2 pints
12 oz = 350 grams   (1 quart)
16 oz   = 1·15 litres
(1 lb) = 450 grams
1¼ lb = 575 grams   1 inch = 2·5 centimetres
1½ lb = 675 grams
1¾ lb = 800 grams
2 lb = 900 grams
2 lb 3 oz
        = 1 kilogram
14 lb
(1 stone)
        = 6·350 kilograms

1 teaspoonful   = 5 millilitres
1 dessertspoonful = 10 millilitres
1 tablespoonful   = 15 millilitres

Note Unless otherwise stated:
All spoon measures are level
All flour is plain flour
Eggs for cakes and puddings are 'average' size

GUIDE TO OVEN TEMPERATURES

	Gas Mark	*°F*	*°C*
	Low	200	100
Very slow	¼	225	110
	½	250	120/30
Slow	1	275	140
	2	300	150
Very moderate	3	325	160/70
Moderate	4	350	180
Moderately hot	5	375	190
Hot	6	400	200
	7	425	220
Very hot	8	450	230
	9	475	240

1. Herbs, Leaves and Flowers

The use of herbs in cookery is mainly for flavouring, but many of the old uses are linked with health and well-being for good reasons, as modern research bears out. Interest and knowledge are widening, and in these days of mass-produced foods and reactions against them home-grown herbs have come back into favour, and wild herbs and plants have become much more sought after—though ironically at a time of real damage, in more ways than ever before, to our countryside.

This chapter begins with well-known culinary herbs and their uses, and goes on to some of the garden and wild plants that have a special place in country cookery and its history.

CULINARY HERBS

Most of them can be home grown quite easily. The herb garden can be a little garden in its own right, or a few plants put in here and there among other plants, or a collection in pots or a window box. There is nearly always a place for it somewhere—the nearer the kitchen, the better.

Sweet herbs is a term used somewhat loosely in cookery, chiefly for a selection of the usual aromatic culinary herbs; sometimes for the sweeter herbs in particular, such as sweet balm (lemon balm) and sweet cicely, which added to stewed fruit can cut down on sugar.

Pot herbs, again a term loosely used, means herbs or plants for the cooking pot, to provide flavour and sometimes substance as well, as in the case of sorrel, which is often called a pot herb. Also, the usual vegetables for flavouring soups and stews. Carrots, turnips and onions are still sometimes called pot herbs by old-fashioned greengrocers.

A faggot of herbs, or a *bunch* or *bouquet* of herbs, means much the same as the French *bouquet garni*, for flavouring soups, stews and meat dishes: generally a bay leaf, one or two sprigs of parsley and a small sprig of thyme, tied together with thread, or in muslin, and removed before serving.

A pinch of herbs should be taken as less than ¼ teaspoonful of (dried) herbs.

A light touch is the right touch, but people's tastes differ widely. Many people do dislike sage, or the aniseed flavour of fennel. Not everyone likes the onion flavour of chives, though it is often preferred to the stronger flavour of onion itself. Some people resent the bits and pieces effect of herbs as a garnish. In many dishes the flavour of herbs is liked best when it is scarcely discernible.

Fresh herbs and dried

Fresh herbs, on the whole, have a finer flavour and more virtue than dried herbs.

Dried herbs are more concentrated in flavour. If substituting fresh herbs for a given amount of dried herbs in a recipe, use two or three times (not more) the amount.

To dry herbs

Most kitchen herbs dry quite well. Sage needs care; dried sage can have a very poor flavour. Chives do not dry well, and parsley becomes rather tasteless, but both these herbs can be frozen quite satisfactorily. A late sowing of parsley sometimes lasts well on into the winter.

The purpose is to preserve the herbs by drying out their moisture without losing too much of the oils which provide their aroma.

The best time to harvest the leaves is just before the plant is ready to flower. Gather on a fine sunny day when the dew has dried, but before the sun has reached its full height. Not in humid weather, and not after rain.

Shake off any dust. Rinse quickly only if necessary, and shake dry very gently in a clean cloth.

When drying the herbs, keep them out of the sun or strong light, in a warm, airy place.

A good old-fashioned method of drying is to tie the stems in small bunches and hang these upside-down in kitchen or attic, or elsewhere, but avoid damp and steam. This method suits the smaller-leaved herbs, such as thyme and marjoram. It also suits lemon balm.

Or the sprigs or leaves can be spread out on muslin or greaseproof paper, preferably over a rack, in a warm but not sunny room; or in a not-too-hot airing cupboard. Turn them now and again. This is the better method for the larger-leaved herbs, such as sage and mint.

Store all dried herbs as soon as perfectly dry—when stems and leaves are brittle and crackly. Rub leaves off the stalks. They can be rubbed through a sieve. They should be left whole if to be used for herb teas.

Store in glass screw-top jars. Not in paper, which gets damp, and not plastic bags. Keep airtight. Avoid exposing the dried herbs to light. Dark glass jars are ideal. Clear glass jars can be kept in an airy cupboard, or brown paper can be tied round the

jar. Label with name and date. Examine soon after storing, and
if there is any sign of moisture in the jar, dry the contents again.
Keep for no more than a year.

Many cookery books now give lists of herbs and their uses.
The following is a short list of herbs with a long tradition in
country cookery, together with a few details that are not
always well known and a few special uses and recipes.

Lemon balm (*Melissa officinalis*)

Sometimes called sweet balm. A popular stewing herb in the
past. Its lemony fragrance is good in stuffings for poultry (or
put a bunch of lemon balm and a small piece of butter into a
chicken for roasting), and in egg or light fish dishes. A few
chopped fresh leaves are excellent in a green salad, especially
when they are mixed with just a hint of very finely chopped
chives. Also good in fruit drinks and fruit salads—it sweetens
slightly. It goes well with rhubarb.

BALM AND RHUBARB

1 lb rhubarb
4 tablespoonfuls sugar
2 or 3 good sprigs lemon balm

I

Wash and trim the rhubarb, do not peel it, cut it across into
small pieces and put into a basin. Cover it with the sugar, stir
it round and leave overnight. Then remove to an enamelled
saucepan, with the lemon balm, washed; add no water, and
stew gently, with the lid on the tilt, until tender. Let it cool in
a basin, uncovered, after removing the balm. It makes a rich

compote. Best chilled. Serve in small pots. The above quantities are for a small amount only.

2

Stew the rhubarb in the usual way, in an enamelled saucepan, with the sugar and ½ pint of water. When done, infuse the sprigs of lemon balm in the hot rhubarb and remove them when it has cooled.

Bay leaves

They should always be leaves from the sweet bay (*Laurus nobilis*), and not from anything else. Garden laurel, with which confusion sometimes arises, is poisonous.

The leaves are mostly used dried (whole, broken or shredded), which brings out their flavour; but use fairly sparingly. Best known in herb bouquets (page 16). A favourite for soups, sauces, stews (beef especially), boiled chicken. Can be used to flavour milk puddings and custards.

Chives (*Allium schoenoprasum*)

Cut them often, leaving a few blades of the 'grass' on each plant. Use fresh from the plant, finely chopped, as a seasoning or a garnish, whenever a mild onion flavour is liked. Specially good in omelets, scrambled eggs, salads, cheese sandwiches, mashed potatoes.

Marjoram

Sweet (or knot) marjoram (*Origanum majorana*), a half-hardy perennial usually treated as an annual, is the most fragrant; but pot marjoram (*Origanum onites*) and wild marjoram (*Origanum vulgare*), perennials, have much the same uses.

Like thyme, with which it is often combined, marjoram has a pervasive flavour and antiseptic qualities also: hence the value of these herbs with meat, especially in days of old. Best in stuffings and various meat dishes. It goes well with stewed woodpigeon. Very well with tomatoes. The fresh leaves can be added to salads.

Mint (*Mentha*)

A herb for the hot days of summer. Fresh bunches of mint used to be hung in kitchen or larder to keep the flies away; which is also an old fisherman's trick and still used sometimes by fish-mongers. Spearmint is the most usual garden mint, but apple-mint is much recommended, and there are several other varieties. The different types are better grown well apart, to avoid cross-pollination. They spread rapidly, and are best planted in containers, sunken (such as an old bucket dug into the ground) or otherwise. For flavouring purposes a little mint goes a long way. For mint sauce see page 67. For mint with new potatoes, adding a sprig of fresh mint (and a small piece of butter) *after* the potatoes are cooked brings out the mint's true fragrance. Fresh mint is also used with green peas, for mint butter (see herb butters, page 25), in salads, for chutney and jellies, in fruit drinks and in sweet dishes, some-times in fillings for pastry.

MINT AND CURRANT PASTY

shortcrust pastry made with 8 oz flour,
    2 oz lard, 2 oz margarine
2 oz butter

1–2 oz sugar
3 oz currants
1–2 tablespoonfuls chopped fresh mint

For the filling, cream the butter and sugar together. Add the currants (about 3 rounded tablespoonfuls) and finely chopped mint (not too much), and mix well. Roll out half the pastry into a rectangle, spread with the filling, damp the edges, cover with the other half of pastry rolled out similarly and press the edges firmly together to seal. Place on a greased baking sheet.

Alternatively it can be made as a plate pie: roll out half the pastry to line a greased pie plate; fill and cover, sealing well, and stand the plate on a baking sheet when it goes into the oven.

The top can be brushed with milk. Prick once or twice with a fork to let out the steam. Bake for about 20 minutes, till golden, in a hot oven (Mark 6, 400 °F).

Parsley (*Carum petroselinum*)

Our most widely used herb, and more than useful—it is so rich in vitamins (A, B and C) and minerals, and aids the appetite and digestion, as well as enhancing many dishes. It goes well with other herbs and can be used fairly freely. Its main uses for flavouring and garnishing are well known. For parsley sauce see page 64, and for parsley butter see herb butters (page 25). Parsley often gets gritty and dusty and so should be very well washed, and then carefully patted dry in a cloth before it is chopped. It is a biennial, and likes a warm soil. Slow to germinate: hence the sayings about it going to the devil and back before starting. The country custom of pouring boiling water along the drills just before sowing helps to provide the warmth and moisture it likes. But why the other old saying, I wonder, that it flourishes only where the missus is master?

Rosemary (*Rosmarinus officinalis*)

The herb of remembrance and friendship. An evergreen shrub and, as with lavender, it is important to cut the latest young growth hard back, straight after flowering is over. Chiefly used with roast meat, lamb especially: just a sprig or two, tucked into or laid on the joint. Can be used with stews, and baked or boiled ham. The warm pine-scented flavour is apt to be over-powering, so use sparingly and always remove before serving. The old wood must never be used, or there will be a strong suggestion of turpentine. Rosemary used to be a flavouring for cakes, jams and jellies. Rosemary sugar, for cakes and milk puddings, is almost forgotten.

ROSEMARY SUGAR

Put 1 or 2 clean and dry sprigs of rosemary and some castor sugar, leaving some space, into a screw-top jam jar. Shake it up, leave overnight. Shake again, and leave aside for a week. Remove the sprigs carefully. Try it in a plain cake mixture.

Sage (*Salvia officinalis*)

The taste of sage can be very obtrusive, so always use carefully. Preferably use freshly gathered. When dried, it often has an inferior flavour. Dried sage (except for sage tea) is usually powdered. Sage and onion stuffing (page 88) for pork or duck counteracts the richness, as well as providing its own special flavour (but not everyone likes it!). Sage can be used when cooking liver, also pork chops, and a little is added with apple to old-fashioned pork stews. In some farmhouses sage was put into a cheese, sometimes a cheese for Christmas time. Derby sage cheese (page 115) is fairly widely sold now, and is sometimes recommended for a cheese sauce.

Thyme (*Thymus vulgaris*)

I think this must be my favourite, with the sense it gives of sunny banks and sun-warmed rocks and stones. Loved by the bees. Very aromatic in stews and soups, and in stuffings and forcemeats. Lemon thyme has a good fragrance for stuffings.

Among other good herbs to grow are salad burnet (*Sanguisorba minor*), a salad herb, very pretty, hardier than it looks, with leaves that taste faintly of cucumber; and winter savory (*Satureia montana*), a good stewing herb if used sparingly; it is like a tiny shrub, darkish green, with a warm but not too strong flavour.

Herbs are full of character, and still partly shrouded in mystery. In the past, country people were much better acquainted with them than we are. They kept them close at hand, indoors and out, brushed against them for fragrance, relied on herb remedies, drank herb teas, made herb cheeses, herb sandwiches. Some herb recipes are given below. For herb teas see Drinks and Remedies (pages 169–70).

Herb cheeses

Mainly for use as cheese spreads. The herbs are chopped finely. Either mix one or two chosen herbs (for example chives and/or parsley) with cream cheese or cottage cheese (page 118); or use grated cheese and a mixture of several herbs in the following way.

HERB CHEESE (MIXED HERBS)

2 dessertspoonfuls mixed herbs (see below)
4 oz Cheddar cheese (or according to choice)
2 tablespoonfuls thin cream
2 dessertspoonfuls sherry (optional)
small piece of butter (about ½ oz)
very little salt and pepper

This is for just a small quantity. Preferably use fresh herbs (otherwise good dried ones, 1 dessertspoonful only): sage, thyme, parsley, chives, perhaps chervil. Chop very finely. Grate the cheese. Put everything together into a double saucepan, or a heat-proof basin over a pan of hot water, and stir with a wooden spoon over a gentle heat until pale green and creamy. Put into little pots. Let it cool. Then it can be used straight away (it should be used soon if sherry omitted) or covered and kept for a few days in a cool place.

Herb sandwiches

The country custom of eating fresh herbs on bread and butter or in special herb sandwiches was partly because they provided some flavour and partly for health and vitality. (Rue sandwiches were strictly medicinal, but are best avoided.) Parsley sandwiches are still popular, and parsley can be added to various other sandwich fillings; so can other suitable herbs. A few marjoram leaves go well with meat or tomato sandwiches; chives with cheese sandwiches; salad burnet with cucumber sandwiches. There are numerous possibilities.

Herb butters

These also are useful for sandwiches; or to serve with grilled fish or meat, or cooked vegetables. They turn a little precious butter into a speciality. Mint butter was liked for meat sandwiches. Parsley butter is better known as *maître d'hôtel* butter. Chives make another good choice; or a few mixed fresh green herbs can be blended together. The usual quantities are about 1 teaspoonful of the finely chopped herb (1 dessertspoonful for parsley) to 1 oz butter. Add a hint of salt and pepper, a few drops of lemon juice, and work all well together. Keep in a cold place.

LEAVES

Some of the plants in this section come under the heading of herbs, though they are more often called weeds. Nettles and dandelions, for example, are attacked as weeds on the one hand; yet as herbs growing wild such plants have a long tradition of use in the countryside—partly through bitter necessity because they are edible, and partly because wisely used they are health-giving. The old word 'wholesome', for 'health-giving', occurs in country writings and recipes over and over again.

Today, with a new interest in wild and natural foods gaining way, many of the old country uses are being revived—sometimes over-enthusiastically.

Hints and warnings

Never eat any part of a plant except on double-checked good authority.

Make sure that the plant in question is the plant that you think it is.

Know the land as well as the plant and beware of all forms of pollution, including spraying with poisonous chemicals.

Wash the plants well.

See that children are given very safe rules about picking and eating from garden plants and plants growing wild.

Learn and see that children learn to recognize the poisonous plants. Deadly nightshade, though the name is well known, is not nearly widely enough recognized. It often grows in gardens. In the garden, also, lily of the valley, aconite, rhubarb leaves and seed pods of laburnum and lupin are all dangerously poisonous. Potato and tomato plants are to some extent poisonous even though the 'root' of potatoes and the fruit of tomatoes are edible. These are only a few of the common plants that are poisonous in one way or another.

Choose young leaves, the earlier the better, as they then have more goodness and a much finer flavour. This is why in country lore and literature we get the true note of delight in all the first green things of spring—coming after the rigours of winter. Also a note of medical fervour for spring soups and salads, teas and tonics, to 'purify the blood' and restore energy when it is at a low ebb. The uses of green leaves and herbs have been summed up quite recently by John Wyatt in *The Shining Levels* (see Acknowledgements), describing a forest life in the Lake District: 'I had some cookery books to help out: one was a battered gem which included wild foods and flavourings with its ingredients. A stew for instance, with jack-by-the-hedge (or garlic-mustard) leaves to give a subtle country flavour. Tansy pudding: made with breadcrumbs, milk and eggs, and chopped tansy leaves. And a traditional dish of the Lake District: 'Easter ledgers', a tasty physic for the countrymen of the pre-can and freezer days, who lived on a winter diet of salt pork, bacon and cereals. This was made from any of the first spring greens such as cabbage leaves, cauliflower or broccoli sprigs, or brussels sprouts tops; and to these were added first and foremost the fresh green leaves of ledgers (bistort), which gave the fine subtle flavour; young nettle leaves, watercress; gooseberry and raspberry leaves new burst; mint, sour docks, jack-by-the-hedge, and a few dandelion leaves. These should be washed and chopped finely, a handful of barley added; and the whole tied into a cloth to simmer in a pan until the liquid is nearly gone. Turn out, add a knob of butter, salt and pepper, and you have a rich dish to make you fighting fit!'

Some of the plants in this quotation are listed below.

Easter ledgers (bistort) (*Polygonum bistorta*)

Sometimes called Easter ledges. Found mainly in Westmoreland and also in some other parts of the north. Spinach can be used instead. The version given above is typical of sundry old recipes, all rather vague, for herb puddings made with barley or oatmeal.

Tansy (*Tanacetum vulgare*)

Grows wild in the north, and elsewhere. Easily grown in the garden. An old medicinal herb. It is said to taste gingery—perhaps more like eucalyptus. It is also said to be poisonous if used in excess, but a beneficial herb if used sparingly. The tansy pudding mentioned above is, again, associated with Easter. The following is a simple version, meant to be served cold with cream, but it can be eaten hot.

TANSY PUDDING

½ pint milk
2 oz fresh white breadcrumbs
2 eggs
2 tablespoonfuls granulated sugar
1–2 teaspoonfuls chopped fresh tansy leaf
½ oz butter

Heat the milk, pour it over the crumbs. Let it stand for ½ hour.
Beat up the eggs, adding the sugar mixed with very finely
chopped tansy leaf. Then mix all well together. Put into a
buttered pie dish. Scatter the butter, in little pieces, on top.
Bake in a moderately hot oven (Mark 4, 350 °F) for ½ hour.
Serve at once, or serve cold with cream.

Gooseberry leaves, raspberry leaves, and blackcurrant leaves

These leaves were used, when very young, for herb puddings
(see above), but blackcurrant leaves are also associated with
more delicate recipes. The following blackcurrant leaf recipe,
from Scotland, was contributed by Mrs. R. Johnstone to
Farmhouse Fare (see Acknowledgements). Half quantities serve
4–6 people.

BLACKCURRANT LEAF CREAM

'Blackcurrant leaves are most delicately scented in the spring
and then is the time to use them for flavouring sweets and all
kinds of creams and puddings.

'This is my own special recipe: Boil 1 lb white sugar with

½ pint water and a cupful of *young* blackcurrant leaves. Boil, without stirring, for 15 minutes; then strain and pour the hot syrup *very gently* on to 2 beaten egg whites. Beat all the time, until the mixture begins to thicken; then stir in the juice of a lemon and a gill of whipped cream.

'Served in individual glasses, it is the most delicious sweet.'

Dandelion (*Taraxacum officinale*)

'Very wholesome.' Tonic and cleansing. The French call it *pissenlit*, which indicates do not use it excessively. All parts of the plant have their uses.

The flowers, freshly gathered, were used for dandelion wine.

The roots from mature plants can be chopped, and roasted in a slow oven, and then ground, to make substitute coffee. This is probably a tedious process.

The young leaves went into herb puddings (see above), and into green soups (page 50), and were sometimes boiled like spinach—sometimes with the tap root as well, if small, but not hair roots and flower buds—and served as a vegetable. They reduce considerably in the cooking. They were often used raw —sometimes again with the tap root as well—either for salads (page 52) or chopped and eaten with bread and butter, as many green herbs were.

Always wash the leaves well. They are bitter and the more so as they get older. If the plant is blanched under a flower pot, the young leaves are sweeter, though rather less health-giving. If forced in this way, they are useful in the early part of the year.

Stinging nettle (*Urtica dioica*)

The common stinging nettle was often used in herb beer, and herb puddings (see above), also with beef stock and barley for nettle broth, or plain boiled as a vegetable. Rich in minerals, iron included. Pick little young shoots only. Use scissors, and wear leather gloves. Wash the shoots well. Boiling water does away with the sting. Cooked like spinach, they tend to taste like boiled cotton wool. Onion is meant to improve them; or butter and lemon juice.

Sorrel

English sorrel (*Rumex acetosa*), sometimes known as sour dock, is a familiar weed, but take care to identify it correctly. Note also that it contains oxalic acid and should be eaten only sparingly. The leaves, finely chopped, add sharpness to salads and soup. For an old-fashioned country green sauce for cold meat they were mashed with a little vinegar and some brown sugar.

French or buckler-leaved sorrel (*Rumex scutatus*), sometimes grown in the garden for culinary use and very good used for soup as in France, has similar properties but a more delicate flavour.

Watercress (*Nasturtium*—botanical names can be very confusing—*officinale*)

Growing wild, it is liable to be contaminated by liver fluke, a dangerous parasite. The safest advice is to eat it only when it has been grown in special watercress beds. It is rich in minerals. Fresh and raw it is much more beneficial than when it is cooked, and May and June are the best months. Watercress is very good added finely chopped to potato soup, right at the last, and it is also a good leaf to use for a green sauce.

GREEN SAUCE

There are two main kinds of country green sauce, made with

watercress, sorrel, any suitable soft green leaves, spinach included, well rinsed and dried. One when the leaves, chopped finely and crushed, are added to a plain white sauce as for parsley sauce (page 64). The other when the leaves (sometimes slightly cooked down or wilted in boiling water) are chopped or pounded, with oil and/or vinegar added (sometimes salt and/or sugar, and then vinegar), and stirred with a wooden spoon.

Nasturtium (*Tropaeolum majus*)

The popular garden annual. Rich in vitamin C, but there is a note of caution that the leaves should be eaten only quite sparingly.

Young green seeds and small buds can be pickled and substituted for capers in a plain white sauce, for much the same uses as onion sauce (page 65). The pickling recipes vary and tend to be sketchy.

The young leaves can be eaten in salads, or with bread and butter, and their peppery flavour is usually rather enjoyed. Their bitterness can pervade other food—eat them straight after preparing them.

The flowers can also be eaten in salads (page 53).

Scented-leaved geranium (*Pelargonium*)

The leaves are used for their fragrance, depending on preference and which particular scent the plant has: orange, lemon, apple, peppermint, rose (a favourite)—there are many varieties. They are often used to flavour apple or crab apple jelly. Add a few leaves to the fruit at the last when it is being cooked for the jelly, then take them out. A leaf or two can be infused in the milk for a custard, or put into a rice pudding before it goes into the oven. To flavour a sponge cake, place a leaf at the bottom of the tin, before baking. Remove the leaf afterwards. Eat the cake soon.

FLOWERS

Some of the edible flowers have special uses for decorating food and for flavouring, though some of these customs may seem a little rarefied and time-consuming for the present day. Also some of the 'perfumed' recipes, which were so much prized in the past, might now seem too scented. Rose petal jams can be cloying, and extravagant on the sugar. Lavender sugar, which is made with lavender flowers in the same way as rosemary sugar (page 22), is now mainly a curiosity. However, for those who like to collect them there are many different flower uses and recipes. For flowers in salads see page 53.

Primroses, violets, roses

Primrose and sweet violet petals were used for garnishing salads (page 53). The flowers were candied or crystallized for cake decoration, as were rose petals. Sometimes Easter biscuits (page 160), set out on their plate, were decorated with a small bunch of primroses. There are various rose and violet recipes for syrups and conserves.

Cowslips

I would love to try cowslip pudding and cowslip wine, and cowslip tea is said to be very soothing, with a beautiful fragrance; but the plants are becoming so rare that they should certainly be left undisturbed.

Elderflowers

Still to be found in abundance. The elder tree has associations with witches (or as a safeguard against them) and it was thought unlucky to cut it. The cream-coloured flowers in their floating shapes are ready at much the same time as the gooseberries, with which their scent most subtly combines to give the flavour of muscatel grapes. For gooseberry and elderflower jam see below; and one or two flower-heads can also be put in with the gooseberries when these are being stewed for a compote or a gooseberry fool. They are also used for elderflower wine or 'champagne', as well as for elderflower water for the complexion, and elderflower ointments and creams. Elderflowers make a very good tea (see herb teas, page 170).

GOOSEBERRY AND ELDERFLOWER JAM

To each 1 lb green gooseberries allow 1 lb sugar, about ½ pint water, and 3 or 4 good heads of elderflowers.

Top and tail the fruit and put it into the pan. Add the water, and the flowers tied loosely in muslin. Simmer until the fruit is soft and you can smell the flower-fragrance. Remove the flowers then. Add the sugar, stir till dissolved. Then boil quite hard, stirring often, until setting point. Skim. Pot and cover.

Marigold

This means the common garden marigold (*Calendula officinalis*), sometimes called pot marigold because it was used for flavouring broths and stews. Use petals only. They can be used fresh or dried. If the petals are pulled off the flowers and spread out on paper in a warm place away from the light, they should keep their colour and dry well. The petals from one or two flowers

B

(or say one or two teaspoonfuls), put into the stew together with the usual culinary herbs, are especially good in a beef stew. In the past marigold petals were used for colouring and flavouring cheeses. They can be used instead of saffron, to give a golden colour and their own special flavour. Chopped petals, a tablespoonful or more, fresh or dried, can be added to mixtures for buns or small cakes. Fresh petals are excellent in salads (page 53).

Nasturtium flowers

Already mentioned above, these were a favourite for salads (page 53).

2. Vegetable Cookery and Salads

VEGETABLE COOKERY

Not all the old ways are the best ways. Green vegetables especially were often boiled far too long and in far too much water, in the belief that lightly cooked they were 'unwholesome'. Also they were often soaked far too long before cooking. In the end, they would have lost much of their goodness.

Fresh vegetables, morning gathered ideally, are best prepared just before use. To boil, cook them quickly, in the smallest amount of water and with the lid on the pan, only just until tender; then dish up and serve straight away, so that as far as possible their vitamins and mineral salts are retained.

Avoid bicarbonate of soda; and there is really no need for the little spoonfuls of sugar that were once the custom to bring out the flavour.

Vegetable water can be used at once for gravy or sauce, or kept for a day or two as stock for sauces or soup. Vegetable trimmings can be chopped up and boiled, for about 20 minutes, for stock.

Dark green outer leaves are rich in food value and should not be cast aside unless unusable.

Medium-sized vegetables are better in flavour and texture than outside 'prize specimens'.

Most vegetables keep best when spread out in a cool, darkish, airy place.

The following notes are on special ways with well-known

vegetables and dried vegetables, vegetable hot-pots and soups.

Artichokes (Jerusalem)

Hard to clean because of being so knobbly. Scrub and rinse well. Scrape or peel and put immediately into cold water with a dash of lemon juice or vinegar to keep them white; or they can be boiled unpeeled and then slipped out of their jackets. Allow 20–30 minutes for boiling, prevent from going too soft, test with a fork, drain at once; serve with white sauce, or mashed with butter and milk. Good roasted (about 45 minutes) in hot fat in a baking tin, or round the joint. They make a very good soup (page 50).

Asparagus

Much more common in the past than the luxury it is now. Must be very freshly cut, the stalk end soft and white, the heads straight. Can be overrated unless beautifully cooked, tied in even bunches and standing upright in a tall pan, so that the stalks cook mainly in the boiling water, the heads in steam; then eaten in the fingers and dipped into just-melted butter.

Broad beans

Use as young as possible. Can be boiled with a sprig of summer (or winter) savory to flavour, and finished with butter and a sprinkling of finely chopped savory and/or parsley. Or serve plain-boiled with parsley sauce (page 64)—the traditional accompaniment to boiled bacon.

The following northern farmhouse dish, from Peggy Hutchinson's *Old English Cookery* (see Acknowledgements), has its own touch of subtlety.

BOILED BEANS AND HAM OR BACON
'broad beans   gammon or bacon slices

Shell the beans, add a little salt and cover with boiling water. Simmer gently until they are tender. Fry slices of ham or bacon and put the resultant fat and the meat on a serving dish. Drain the beans and serve together with the ham.

The broad beans should be picked before the brown speckles show on the pod. The ham is sliced thinly—not as some grocers slice it, in half-inch layers, fondly believing they are cutting ham as it should be cut. We farmers know different, and call these ham steaks "bull's lugs".'

French and runner beans

Top and tail with a sharp knife and remove 'string' from ribs if necessary. Cook whole if young and small; otherwise in halves or short lengths, and the old rule was never cut them up with a knife, but break them by hand. This gives a much better flavour. If they are fresh they break easily.

Beetroot

To boil raw beetroot whole, cut off some of the stalk, wash off all the earth, but do not bruise the skin or root or it will bleed. If this happens, the advice is to dip it into dry flour before boiling. I am not very fond of beetroot, but I have lists of its uses and the herbs and spices that go with it: basil, caraway, cinnamon, coriander, fennel and savory. It can be baked, boiled, fried, pickled, and even made into jam, and I have a recipe for a beetroot pie, but I don't think I would like it. The following is a quick way of serving it hot.

QUICK HOT BEETROOT

Skin and slice ready-boiled beetroot, heat through in barest amount of boiling water, drain, then add butter, a few drops of vinegar, salt and pepper.

To store. Beets are stored like carrots, but the rule is don't cut off the leaves, twist them off with both hands (though this is not always so easy).

Broccoli

Usually treated like cauliflower. It is hardier than the cauliflower, and has become very popular. Boil quickly with the lid off the pan and drain as soon as done, to prevent discoloration. The small shoots of the sprouting varieties, lightly cooked, are very tender and full of vitamins.

Brussels sprouts

The best vegetable of all for the Christmas roast turkey. When preparing remove as few outside leaves as possible, cut a little cross at the base. When cooking, take particular care to put them into fast boiling water, so that they keep their colour. Best served plain boiled or lightly tossed in butter or margarine. A touch of nutmeg is the traditional flavouring, if wished. They can be served as a slightly buttery purée, or roughly mashed, and are good combined with boiled chestnuts.

A frost makes them 'brisker', but a lot depends on the soil in which they are grown.

Cabbage

The main cause of complaints about bad English cookery. The best way to boil it is to cut the cabbage in halves or quarters, wash it quickly in salted water, and shred it with a sharp knife, discarding the stalk if too thick; then boil it lightly in a strong covered pan with as little boiling water or meat stock as possible and a little salt. It should not take long. Watch it well. Drain thoroughly and serve at once. It can be tossed in butter or margarine, and a little vinegar can be added or some grated nutmeg and/or pepper. A crust of bread in the pan was the old way to keep down the smell, but with quick cooking and modern kitchens this is not such a problem.

For bubble and squeak, and colcannon, see under potatoes, below.

Carrots

Rich in vitamin A. Very useful for flavour and colour in soups and stews, and very adaptable. For boiled or braised carrots, chopped parsley is the favourite garnish. Chopped chives can go well, and good sauces (see the chapter on Sauces) are parsley sauce, cheese sauce, white sauce with a little ground nutmeg.

Carrot jam was a wartime standby. In the north especially, grated carrot sometimes goes into a fruit cake and is quite a usual ingredient in a plum pudding (page 141).

Carrots feature in various supper dish recipes, but in some of them the amount of chopped carrot can be overpowering.

To store. Do not clean; cut off leaves to 1 inch. Pack in sand or soil, not too dry, in box or crate. Cover with sacking or straw. Keep in a cool frost-proof place.

Cauliflower

'Sit it up' in the pan so that the flower head is clear of the boiling water and cooks in steam. Some of the older recipes advocate boiling it upside down, to avoid discoloration and to enable it to be turned right way up on to the saucepan lid after draining, for easier dishing up, but in this way the flower head is usually overcooked. To cook quickly, divide into sprigs. It can be served with butter or margarine melted over it; or coated with a good white sauce, made with milk and cauliflower stock and flavoured with a hint of nutmeg or mace or some grated cheese.

CAULIFLOWER CHEESE

Boil the cauliflower lightly, put it into a baking-dish, cover well with cheese sauce and sprinkle with a grating of extra cheese. Then brown under the grill, or for a few minutes in a hot oven.

Celery

Best from autumn to early spring. Usually liked raw, with cheese. Not always so much liked when it is cooked, but braising suits it well, with some onion; or it can be baked with salt, pepper, mace and onion, then tossed in a little very strong meat stock or served with a brown gravy sauce.

Cucumber

Cooked cucumber recipes used to be rather popular.

FRIED CUCUMBERS

Peel (unless it is young) and slice a long cucumber, dust the slices with pepper and flour, fry them lightly in hot dripping or butter, adding a little salt just before they are done.

STEWED CUCUMBERS

Proceed just as above, but fry a sliced onion as well if you wish. Then add about a gill of good stock and gently cook and stir for 5 minutes.

Kale (or kail)

The word comes from the Gaelic. Much used in Scottish and Irish cookery. For colcannon see under potatoes, below. Kale can be grown in poor soils and is very hardy indeed, and useful when other green vegetables are scarce and expensive. Strip leaves from stalks, unless it is very young, and boil as for cabbage, serving with plenty of butter.

Leeks

A first favourite. With crisp bacon, cheese sauce, browned breadcrumbs, or in 'puddings' (the white part, chopped, with a suet crust) or pies, they make excellent dishes in their own right. Very useful for soups and broths.

To clean: After removing the roots, and the coarse outer leaves and tops, cut the leeks in half lengthways and wash through and through under cold running water.

Lettuce

Lettuces were quite often boiled, and sometimes served with white sauce. Braising gives them more flavour.

BRAISED LETTUCE

A good method when lettuces are prolific. Cut them in half, if small, or else separate the leaves. Wash, shake dry, then sweat the lettuce in butter. After that, add a little good stock and cook covered, say 10–15 minutes, and watch for burning. Like spinach, it will boil down considerably. Let the liquid boil nearly away. Add a few drops of lemon juice if wished. Serve very hot.

Mushrooms

In the past they were carefully cleaned with salt and a piece of flannel. They were cooked, upturned, with the cups sprinkled with salt, either in the oven in saucers of cream or simply placed on top of the stove; or they were shaken in a little hot butter in a heavy pan, then stewed gently, their own juice providing far the best flavour, but besides salt and pepper a little ground mace was sometimes liked as a seasoning. Sometimes they were dried, strung on thread, and then were usually powdered (Eliza Acton points out that the powder must be kept perfectly dry or it could become putrid). Sometimes big mushrooms were salted until the juice ran, which was then boiled with spices for ketchup.

Mushrooms go well in beef stews. They go extremely well with woodpigeon, and are good with any rather dry meat, game or poultry. The big flat mushrooms are delicious cut up and fried in the fat from the bacon. Field mushrooms, that spring up in the misty pastures like magic, are the finest for flavour but have now become rare.

Avoid reheating left-over cooked mushrooms. Field mushrooms especially should be used when very fresh, and eaten freshly cooked. If the skin will not peel off easily, it may not be a mushroom at all. If mushrooms are young they need not always be peeled, but can just be wiped. Always cut off and discard the earth end of the stalk.

Onions

They have a great reputation among country people for curing colds and chills (page 172). English onions give a good pungent flavour to broths and stews. Spanish onions are milder and sweeter for using raw (page 52) and for the numerous onion savouries that make economical supper dishes (see cheese and onion pie, page 116).

For onion sauce see page 65, and for sage and onion stuffing page 88. Fried onions go well with liver and bacon, and small baked onions go well with roast duck. The green shoots that sprout from stored onions can be chopped up and used as a flavouring. Onion skins give a golden colour to hard-boiled eggs dyed for Easter (page 101).

To peel: Peeling under cold water helps prevent smarting eyes. Slice quickly on a flat plate, using a very sharp knife. Rinse hands, knife and plate in cold water so that the onion smell does not linger.

To store. String them up, or sling up in a net, and hang in an airy place.

Parsnips

Much grown as a cottage vegetable in the past. Probably their favourite use then was for parsnip wine. There are some quite elaborate old recipes for making the best of them, but usually rather extravagant. Boiled, they can taste unattractively sweetish and woolly. They can be mashed with a little butter. Cut into wedges and roasted till brown, they are better.

Peas

When they are really young, small and fresh, nothing improves on their flavour, not even the traditional sprig of mint (sometimes a spring onion instead) and little spoonful of sugar. They should be gently simmered, with just a pinch of salt, in water barely to cover.

To test: Dig a thumb-nail into the pod, and the sap will start if the peas are fresh.

Potatoes

All the general cookery books give detailed instructions for potato cookery, which is an art in itself. Irish recipes, also some of the Lancashire ways, are especially good. The following notes are at random.

Potatoes are much better-flavoured and more nutritious if cooked (boiled, baked or steamed) in their skins. When they have to be peeled, peel them thinly.

When potatoes are boiled without their skins, 'shaking the pan in the wind' (or in a draught) when they are done helps to make them white and floury.

For mashed potatoes, a potato masher or ricer is helpful, and also a wooden spoon. Milk and butter or margarine are usually added, but the mashed potato can quite well be 'made smooth' just with milk.

Turn and baste roast potatoes when cooking them round a

joint, or in hot fat in a separate tin, so that they brown and crisp well. Note that in country recipes potatoes baked in their jackets are sometimes referred to as 'roast potatoes', which can be confusing.

Potatoes baked in their jackets were often served in a folded napkin, to keep them hot and absorb the steam.

For mint with new potatoes see page 20.

When cutting peeled potatoes in pieces to thicken a stew, or meat pie or similar dish, do not cut through but 'crack off' the pieces instead, to give a rough edge.

Slice peeled potatoes thinly for the top layer of a hot pot so that they will be slightly curled, crisp and brown.

Freshly cooked potatoes are better than 'left-overs' for all 'made up' potato dishes. See cottage pie, page 78. Boiled potatoes soon deteriorate, and should not be kept for more than 24 hours.

Bubble and squeak is made with mashed potato and chopped cooked cabbage, mixed together and fried brown, shaped as a large flat cake, in hot dripping.

Colcannon is made with mashed potato mixed with chopped cooked kale (but cabbage is often used) and a little milk, with leeks or onion to flavour. The kale or cabbage is beaten in last and the mixture, which should be fluffy and green, is made very hot in a saucepan, piled on to a dish, and eaten with butter, melted into a well in the centre.

Potato pastry is useful for savoury dishes. Proportions vary, but say 3 oz margarine, 4 oz sieved boiled potatoes, 5 oz flour, 1 teaspoonful of baking powder, ½ teaspoonful of salt. No water. Soften the margarine, add the other ingredients and mix to a stiff dough. Knead and roll out lightly on a lightly floured board. This quantity can be used for an 8-inch plate pie. Stewing steak, cooked, then cooled and chopped small with gravy added, makes a good filling. Bake in a hot oven (Mark 6, 400 °F), watching for burning, for ½ hour.

Potato cakes (many recipes) are excellent fried with bacon or eaten as hot scones with butter.

Potato puddings appear among old-fashioned pudding recipes; not all of them are particularly economical. For potato in plum pudding, with carrot, see page 141.

To store. Potatoes should be kept in a cool, dark, dry, airy, frost-proof place. They should be sound and dry. Clean off clods of earth, but do not wash. Spread them out loosely, or pack into a wooden crate (it can be lined with straw or newspaper), or they can be put into a sack. Making an outdoor clamp, for storing large quantities, needs demonstration. The clamp should be ventilated.

Note that new potatoes are immature and should be used soon.

Spinach

As it boils down so considerably, allow ½ lb for each person. Clean and cook with great care. Remove thick stalks and coarse ribs and wash it in a big china bowl, in several changes of water. Boil it lightly in scarcely any water at all in a big heavy pan with a lid. Shake the pan now and again. Drain and press well. Butter marvellously brings out the flavour. For creamed spinach, add a little white sauce (page 63) or thick cream. For a lighter result, add whipped egg white instead. Season with salt and pepper, and a pinch of ground mace or nutmeg if wished. Fried bread, but it should be crisp, sometimes accompanies it. For poached eggs on spinach see page 96.

Swedes (Swedish turnip)

Peel them thickly, like turnips. Cut into pieces and boil until tender and golden. When cooked they can be tossed in butter or margarine. They are usually mashed, sometimes together with carrots. Swedes go well with sausages and/or bacon.

SWEDE AND BACON

Roughly chop some boiled swede. Pile it very hot into a dish and add pieces of fried streaky bacon, letting the fat run well in.

Tomatoes

Raw, fresh-picked tomatoes are best for flavour and vitamins. For cooked tomatoes, the quick simple ways are to serve them baked, grilled or fried, with bacon, eggs, sausages, liver, kidneys, steaks, chops, cutlets, mushrooms; also with fish, or in their own right on hot buttered toast. Sliced tomatoes sometimes went into farmhouse meat pasties. For savoury dishes, tomatoes combine well with cheese, onion, browned breadcrumbs. Good herbs with them are basil and marjoram, sage sometimes, and parsley. For 'full fries', fry them last because of their wateriness.

To skin: Dip into boiling water for $\frac{1}{2}$ minute, then into cold water immediately, and then slip off the skin.

Turnips

One of the 'pot herbs' for flavouring soups and stews, but they have a reputation for turning stock sour in hot weather. The traditional vegetable to cook and serve with boiled mutton. Homely turnip dishes were held in affection. The following is a simpler dish than the ones finished off in the oven with breadcrumbs.

A GOOD TURNIP DISH

Prepare and slice the turnips. Boil them lightly. Drain well, and leave them in the pan. Add a dash of creamy milk, a scrap of butter and a little grated cheese. Stir round and mash roughly over a very low heat. Serve straight away.

Boiled turnips are excellent roughly mashed with boiled carrots. A farmhouse way with mashed turnips was to add thick cream and white pepper. Young turnip tops are highly nutritious. They can be boiled in the usual way for green vegetables for about 15 minutes.

Vegetable marrow

Small or medium-sized marrows are better for vegetable cookery than the big prize ones. Fair-sized marrows are often stuffed and baked. The stuffing can be of minced raw meat and/ or skinned tomatoes, with breadcrumbs, herbs and seasonings, including lightly fried chopped onion. An onion flavour is sometimes liked for boiled marrow; a small onion is cooked with the marrow and then removed, or the marrow can be served with a mild onion sauce. Perhaps butter is better.

BUTTERED VEGETABLE MARROW

Choose a medium-sized marrow. Wash it and peel it thinly. Remove seeds and pith. Cut it into not too small pieces. Melt a knob of butter, add the pieces of marrow and stir them round over a very low heat. Then add just a dash of hot water and a sprinkling of salt and pepper. Cover, and cook very gently for say 20 minutes. Shake the pan now and again. Drain (the liquid can be used for a sauce), and serve at once, garnished with finely chopped parsley.

To store: Keep marrows on a shelf, or slung up in a string bag, in a fairly warm place.

Dried vegetables (pulses): beans, peas, split peas, lentils

The following are extra reminders. Do not oversoak. Drain, throw the water away, rinse well, put into fresh cold water, bring to the boil and boil gently. Pulses are rich in protein. They need fat to balance them, and the custom of boiling them with pieces of bacon supplies this. Bacon rinds can be used as a flavouring. Good flavourings for beans and lentils are an onion stuck with a clove, 1 or 2 carrots, a bunch of sweet herbs; for peas and split peas, a sprig of fresh mint or pinch of dried mint, a little sugar.

Vegetable hot pots

These were beloved for using up 'left-overs', but are much better if the vegetables are cooked freshly and not simply reheated. The following is an example.

VEGETABLE HOT POT

Carrots, swedes, turnips, onions, white part of leeks, celery, parsnips if liked, are all good to choose from. Prepare a mixture of vegetables and chop small. Fry lightly in butter or dripping, add salt and pepper, then put into a casserole with enough thin white sauce (page 63), made with water, to mix all well together. Cover the dish and cook in a slow oven (Mark 2, 300 °F) for about 2 hours.

Vegetable soups

They can be fairly delicate, as are the spring and summer soups mentioned below, or more robust. Strong meat stocks or bouillon cubes can spoil the true flavour. Very smooth purées may seem lacking in character; on the other hand, chunks and strands are unwelcome.

Spring soups come into the country tradition of making the most of green things in the springtime, and sometimes have the title green soup. Young green leafy vegetables, herbs and spring onions, are cut up finely, sweated in butter or dripping, simmered gently in white stock or water, thickened to taste, perhaps with milk added, and seasoned, but not too strongly.

Summer soups continue the theme, with young green peas and other young vegetables in season thrown in.

Famous among the more substantial vegetable soups are artichoke soup (made with Jerusalem artichokes and consequently known also as Palestine soup; takes trouble to make, but worth it if time allows; a little mashed potato makes a good thickening); pea soup (made with dried peas and preferably the stock from a ham bone or boiled bacon; garnish with chopped crisp streaky bacon or little cubes of fried bread); potato soup (the plainest versions are best; leek and potato is excellent); onion soup (for cold weather and cold cures; long slow cooking brings out the flavour; French recipes are usually best).

SALADS

As soon as all the green things of spring began to appear,

came the 'salad days'. 'Spring salad' is the title that crops up most frequently among country salad recipes; though there is really not much need for recipes. It is so much a question of what is liked and what is available, and most people have their own ideas.

Small, simple salads, often eaten with bread and butter at tea-time, and big mixed salads to go with cold meats, including brawns, moulds and galantines, mostly in summer, are in the main country tradition. For the latter, a home-made 'salad sauce', based on a thick white sauce (page 63) seasoned with salt, pepper, mustard and sugar, with vinegar added, was probably the most popular dressing. For green salads a simple dressing of salad oil and either vinegar or lemon juice, mixed and seasoned according to taste, is usually best.

The following notes are at random, with salad herbs, flowers and fruit at the end.

Break or tear lettuce rather than cut it, but whole leaves have the best flavour.

As an alternative to garlic, rub the salad bowl round with bruised mint or a piece of spring onion.

Home-grown mustard and cress make good salad sandwiches.

Watercress must be very fresh and from a reliable source (see page 30).

Not everyone likes raw tomatoes. (They took a long time in this country, even in this present century, to become generally popular.)

To prepare cucumber for salads or sandwiches, slice very thin (peeled or not as preferred), sprinkle lightly with salt, leave for about half an hour, drain, and press dry with a tea towel.

Radishes, with bread and butter and salt, are very nice for breakfast.

Grated raw turnip and radish go well with grated raw carrot.

Raw Brussels sprouts, shredded, are very good in salads in winter.

Celery was sometimes eaten at winter tea-times, with hot buttered toast.

Onion for salads

Raw onion, Spanish onions for preference, was much relished with cheese or cold beef, and made a popular salad for winter; in the north of England especially. To make an onion salad, skin the raw onion, slice thin, put the slices in a dish (a glass dish was usual), sprinkle slightly with salt, cover with brown malt vinegar. Leave for an hour or two, or overnight. Sometimes a little oil is mixed with the vinegar, and pepper and sugar.

Dandelion for salads

Dandelion (see previous chapter) was often used for spring salads. The young leaves were added to other green things, or were used to make a small salad in their own right. This was sometimes, as in France, mixed with fried streaky bacon, chopped small, and the hot fat, with a little vinegar, poured straight over the leaves. Dandelion leaves are also good with chopped hard-boiled egg and spring onion, and an oil and vinegar dressing.

Herbs in salads

Freshly picked herbs, usually chopped very finely, add a subtle flavour to salads; they should not be too prevailing. Some good herbs for flavouring salads: lemon balm (excellent), chives (when mild onion flavour is liked)—for lemon balm blended with chives see page 18—chervil (blends well), salad burnet (delicate cucumber flavour), basil (with tomatoes), thyme (very sparingly), marjoram, mint, parsley, tarragon. Also dandelion (astringent), sorrel (sharp), nasturtium leaves (peppery), all of which are mentioned in the previous chapter.

Flowers and fruit in salads

Flower uses are mentioned in the previous chapter. Just the petals are used as a rule, of certain edible flowers, to decorate and add a delicate flavour. Best with lettuce and a simple oil and lemon juice dressing. Primroses and sweet violets were popular. A sprinkling of marigold petals adds a very attractive flavour and colour. Nasturtium flowers are more flamboyant: whole blossoms garnished or even composed the salad and were eaten quite cheerfully. Fruit, just a little, was sometimes put into a farmhouse mixed salad. Sometimes a pear chopped up small, and chopped apple for sharpness and crispness. Chopped raw apple goes well with various salad ingredients, especially with celery. Chopped, unpeeled rosy apples add colour.

3. Fruit: Wild and Orchard

The recipes of Eliza Acton, written in the first half of the nineteenth century, convey the whole art of fruit cookery. Every detail is exactly adjusted to the fruit, its variety and the season, late or early, sunny or rainy.

Gathering

Pick in fine weather, but not if the fruit is still wet after rain; when the dew has dried and the sun is well up. Handle with care to protect the bloom, and to guard against bruising. Set aside any fruit that is damaged or overripe.

Apples and pears are ready for picking when the fruit comes away easily in the hand. In general, the early varieties are eaten soon after picking, and late varieties left to ripen fully in store. Quinces are picked very late, usually mid-November, and then need to mellow in store, perhaps for a few weeks. Plums are picked when quite ripe (but when only just ripe if for jam-making), and damsons just slightly underripe. Cherries also when ripe. Peaches ideally just before eating. Except for green gooseberries for cooking, soft fruits are picked as they ripen.

A word here on rhubarb. Always pull, never cut, and never pull after midsummer (because the oxalic acid content builds up). Never use the leaves, whatever old-fashioned cookery books may say to the contrary; they are poisonous.

Storing

Store only sound fruit. Any that is bruised, overripe or damaged by insects or birds should be used very quickly. Fruit brought in for jamming or bottling should be used straight away.

In the ordinary way keep fruit in a cool, fairly dark, airy place, but if dessert pears or peaches are almost ready for eating, they can be put in the warm to improve. Wooden racks, boards or boxes, chip baskets, or wicker baskets lined with brown paper, are useful for firm fruits. For soft fruits see farther on. Look the fruit over often. Use all fruit as soon as possible, except for hard fruits kept long-term to mature: late apples and pears, and quinces, as follows.

For apples, a clean, well-ventilated cellar is ideal, and if it is a little damp so much the better; otherwise as near to such conditions as possible. As a rule, they keep longer if wrapped in paper. Waxed, greaseproof or brown can be used. Avoid tissue paper. Newspaper can be rather smeary, but is very often used. Pears like a slightly warmer and dryer atmosphere. Opinions differ over whether to wrap them or not. They should be eaten as soon as ready—pears when fully ripe soon go sleepy. Quinces can be rather a problem, especially near other fruit, as their smell is very pervasive.

Soft fruits should be used with the least delay. Remove at once from punnets or bags, sort out at once and remove any that are squashy or mouldy. If in very good condition soft fruit can be left overnight, spread out on greaseproof paper on a plate or dish. To keep overnight if not in such good condition, wash the fruit quickly and drain (hull strawberries first); put into a shallow dish and cover with plenty of sugar, then leave in a cool place. If gooseberries are firm and dry, they can be kept in a cool place for a day or two.

Some hints on preparing

Large fruit, bought fruit especially, should be carefully washed, then dried with a cloth. Small fruit can be washed (quickly) in a basin or jar, then drain the water away through the fingers or a nylon strainer. Repeat once or twice more if necessary. Dessert fruits such as peaches, plums, grapes are not washed unless it is really necessary, as this spoils the bloom.

Peel fruit with a silver or stainless steel knife.

String currants with a fork.

Top and tail gooseberries with scissors.

A corer is useful for apples and pears, and a stoner for cherries.

Apples peel more easily if scalding water is poured over them.

Peaches and plums can be skinned by dipping them into scalding water for a minute; then the skins can be quickly slipped off.

A little lemon juice helps to keep cut fruit from going brown (caused by oxydization).

To prevent the fruit from discolouring, apples and pears peeled for cooking can be put into cold water with a dash of lemon juice, or into salted cold water (1 tablespoonful salt to 1 quart; drain and rinse before use).

Stewed fruit

Always cook the fruit very gently, to bring out the flavour.

Cook covered either on top of the stove or in a slow oven (which can take twice as long).

Use a very clean, sound saucepan or double boiler, or a good oven dish with a lid (a brownware stew jar is good); a wooden spoon for stirring; a nylon sieve or strainer for purées, or beat to a pulp with a wooden spoon.

Add a little but not too much water (very little for very juicy fruits) and sweeten just enough and not heavily.

White sugar (granulated) is generally used. Demerara or soft pale brown sugar (dark brown is rather too strong, except sometimes for rhubarb) can be used instead, for a richer colour and flavour when wanted. So can honey or golden syrup. Sweet cicely and lemon balm (see balm and rhubarb, page 18) flavour and sweeten slightly.

Cooking in a light sugar syrup helps to keep shape and flavour. As a rule, 2–4 oz sugar and ½ pint water to 1 lb fruit. Less water for very juicy fruits such as currants or raspberries; more for very hard fruits. Heat and stir the sugar and water until the sugar dissolves, let it boil for a minute or two; add the fruit, cover, or poach uncovered, watch carefully, simmer gently until tender.

Note that very hard pears—best cooked in a slow oven—can take several hours.

Fruits and traditional flavours

This list shows some of the ways of combining and flavouring particular fruits, especially when used for stewed fruit dishes and other forms of fruit cookery.

Apples. Blackberries, elderberries, plums, damsons, raspberries, quinces, lemon or orange (rind and/or juice), orange marmalade, dried fruit, candied peel, cloves, mixed spice, nutmeg, cinnamon, ginger, cider, a scrap of butter; cheese with raw apples, and according to north country custom with apple pies and tarts.

Gooseberries. Elderflowers (page 33) for the superlative 'muscatel' flavour; sometimes a hint of nutmeg or ginger.

Peaches. Raspberries, lemon juice.

Pears. Apples, plums, a piece of quince when stewing hard pears, lemon or orange, cloves, mixed spice, ginger.

Plums. Apples, mixed spice, cinnamon.

Raspberries. Redcurrants, cinnamon.

Redcurrants. Raspberries.

Rhubarb. Lemon balm (page 18), ginger, nutmeg.

Strawberries. Nothing can improve on fresh strawberries eaten warm from the sun, or 'strawberries, sugar and cream', but otherwise lemon juice, orange juice—or a dash of pepper!

Mixed summer fruits. For a mixture of fresh summer fruits, strawberries, raspberries, cherries and red and white currants all go well together.

Fruit preservation

Before the arrival of the freezer, the main ways were jamming and bottling. For jam-making see page 162. For bottled fruit the principle is to preserve by means of sterilization and sealing. Sugar if used is for better flavour and texture. Detailed instructions are necessary. Some of the old ways for small fruits need no special equipment and can work very well (see bottled blackberries: a north country way, page 60).

Just to mention some other methods of fruit preservation. Candying takes up a great deal of time and is heavy on sugar. Brandying (as for brandied cherries or peaches) and other forms of preserving in alcohol are expensive. Preserving with vinegar includes the pickled and spiced fruit recipes, which most of us have never yet tried but perhaps mean to try one day, and also chutneys in all their variety. Chutneys were made abundantly to eat with cold meat—if also abundant—and as a great way of using up windfalls. They go well with cheese, and are useful for curries. The drawbacks are that they can be fiddly to make, take a long time to cook, and sometimes smell quite disagreeable meanwhile.

For fruit pickles and chutneys a close airtight seal to the jars is essential or the vinegar will soon start to evaporate. Jars with corks are sometimes used. Paraffin wax, from the chemist's, or clarified mutton fat can be melted and poured on to the contents, still hot, to seal the neck of the jar. Preserving-jars with glass tops can be used. Metal is easily corroded by vinegar.

Good fruits for chutneys are apples, damsons, gooseberries, plums, rhubarb, and good recipes are easily collected.

Drying, lastly, is slow and needs plenty of space in the oven. Here are suggestions for apples (windfalls can be used). Peel, core, leaving whole, and cut out damaged parts. Cut into thin rings, putting into salted water to prevent discoloration. Spread on trays in a *very cool* oven. The heat should be no more than 150 °F. Leave to dry, until shrivelled, say 4–6 hours. Watch and turn now and again. To cool, leave spread out in a cool place, 12 hours or longer. When cold, pack into storage jars. To use, soak for at least 24 hours, simmer gently in the same water, adding a little more water if necessary; stir in some sugar towards the end of the cooking time.

Wild and hedgerow fruits

Our wild fruits are a most precious heritage—perhaps some of us realize this all the more, now that so many hedgerow fruits are fast disappearing or being ruined by chemical spraying.

Blackberries (brambles) have long been taken for granted. Good blackberrying places are becoming harder and harder to find, but oh, the joy of a proper blackberrying expedition in

September!—in October the blackberries belong to the devil and there is sense in that saying because the late ones are not good for jam-making. Of all the wild fruits blackberries have the largest number of uses: for wines, jams, jellies, syrups, pies, puddings. They are also a useful fruit to cultivate in the garden. Sometimes they are used together with elderberries or other wild berries. Blackberry and apple is the ideal partnership: each adds to the other.

BLACKBERRY AND APPLE

Quantities as you please, but more apple than blackberry. Stew the apples first, gently, with a little sugar and not too much water, and add the blackberries for a few minutes at the end. Serve hot or cold, with cream or without.

BLACKBERRY AND APPLE FOOL

Cook the fruit as above, in only the barest amount of water, until thick. Strain off any surplus juice. Sieve to a purée. Serve cold, and serve the whipped cream separately, so that it does not cloud the beautiful colour.

BOTTLED BLACKBERRIES: A NORTH COUNTRY WAY

Here is an old way of bottling blackberries for winter, in ordinary jam jars. For experiment, in a slow oven. This recipe is from Peggy Hutchinson, *Old English Cookery* (see Acknowledgements): 'Use glass jam jars but, after washing, these must be baked in the oven to kill all germs and ensure that they are thoroughly dry on the inside. Now fill up with well-picked-over berries, which must have been gathered when the fruit was quite dry. After filling, spread some paper in the oven bottom (this is to prevent the jars from cracking) and place the full jars on the paper. Have the kettle boiling, and when the blackberries change colour and shrink (this takes a good 10 minutes), fill them up with boiling water.

'Cover immediately with stick-on jam covers. If you have none, try this new method. Get greaseproof paper and cut a square big enough to cover the top and come well over the sides of the jar. Wet every bit of it with milk and put the wet side to the top, pressing it well on to the glass sides with the hands. In a short time the paper dries like parchment, sticks well and makes a thoroughly airtight cap; but this method won't do on cold bottles. After the cover is dry, tie over a double thickness of newspaper to finish the job.

'During the winter months, open a jar when required, pour off the water and use the fruit just as you would fresh black-berries. Bottled in this way the fruit will keep all winter.'

Bilberries (blaeberries, whortleberries) are sometimes used in a summer pudding (page 134). They are said to make a good jam with half their weight in either apples or blackberries.

Elderberries are very rough eaten raw, but they add a distinctive flavour and a deep colour when cooked with apples. Not quite so good with pears. They are excellent for wines, jellies, jams (see apple and elderberry jam, page 168), and syrups for hot drinks and cold cures (page 171).

Hips and haws. Rose hips and hawthorn berries have to be gathered determinedly. Apart from rose hip syrup, they are used chiefly for jellies.

Rowan berries (mountain ash berries). They make a bitter jelly for use with game and cold meats.

Wild raspberries. Eat freshly gathered.

Sloes. These are the little dark wild 'plums' of the hedges. They are the fruit of the blackthorn. Once discovered, they are easy to pick in fair quantities, but so bitter they will set your teeth on edge if you bite them. Their famous use was for sloe gin. They can be cooked down with apples and made into jelly or jam (see sloe and apple jelly jam, page 168).

4. Traditional Sauces

Really a very simple tradition, with a rooted distrust of anything fanciful or elaborate.

Butter is preferred in the following recipes, but a good brand of margarine can be used instead.

Note that 'serve with melted butter', in old recipes, may mean with melted butter sauce, which certainly in the nineteenth century was extremely popular. It was usually made with a lot of butter, very little flour, and some water, and sometimes some cream to complete it (the result has to be creamy, not oily), but most of its numerous versions are too rich and extravagant for most purposes nowadays. A simple white sauce became the accepted alternative.

Our usual white sauce (sometimes hopefully equated with the French béchamel) is the basis for several others.

Twelve traditional sauces

WHITE SAUCE (GENERAL PURPOSE)

1 oz butter
½–1 oz flour
½ pint milk (or milk and/or stock)

The milk can be mixed with a little hot water, if wished. Milk and/or stock, such as vegetable, chicken or fish stock, can be used when appropriate.

Melt the butter in a saucepan until it starts foaming, add the flour (about 1 rounded tablespoonful), stir and cook for a minute or two without browning, add the liquid (hot but not boiling) gradually, stirring well. Add more liquid if a thin sauce is needed; use less liquid for a very thick sauce. Boil gently, still stirring, for 5 minutes or so. Add salt and pepper (or if wished a teaspoonful of sugar for a pudding sauce) and extra flavouring if required. For extra smoothness and flavour a tiny piece of butter can be stirred in, off the heat, at the end.

CHEESE SAUCE

To ½ pint of white sauce (see above) add ½–1½ oz (2–6 table-spoonfuls) grated cheese. Melt it in, without boiling. Add a touch of made mustard if liked. For browned dishes such as cauliflower cheese (page 40) keep back some of the cheese for sprinkling on top.

For fish, egg and vegetable dishes.

EGG SAUCE

Hard boil 1 or 2 eggs, chop roughly, stir them into ½ pint of white sauce (see above). Fish stock or chicken stock can be combined with milk for the sauce, depending on use.

Now used mainly for fish; but it was a favourite sauce for boiled fowl, hot or cold, and for this purpose an excellent version is made with half milk, half stock from the boiling fowl, plus chopped parsley.

PARSLEY SAUCE

For a creamy-white sauce clearly speckled with green, strip parsley from stems, chop fairly finely, and after that rinse it well in a cloth. Add it to the hot sauce, allowing 1–2 table-spoonfuls of parsley to ½ pint of white sauce (see above), and stir round over a low heat without boiling, just for a minute. Serve straight away.

For fish, all kinds of boiled meats, and broad beans with boiled bacon.

ONION SAUCE

Peel and chop a large onion, Spanish onion for preference. Boil it in slightly salted water till soft. Drain well, chop it finer (by careful cooks in the past it was sieved) and add to ½ pint of white sauce (see above). Add salt and pepper. Some cooks add nutmeg. Serve hot.

This went with roast shoulder of mutton, but it can be served with roast lamb. Also for boiled mutton and lamb, and boiled rabbit.

MUSTARD SAUCE

At its simplest, 1 teaspoonful or more of made mustard to ½ pint white sauce (see above), salt and pepper to taste. Serve hot.

Some recipes include vinegar, a teaspoonful or two, either mixed with dry mustard or added to the sauce separately; and some people then find they like to add sugar, a pinch or two, to round off the flavour.

For herrings and mackerel. Also good mixed with chopped ham and served on hot buttered toast.

BREAD SAUCE

    4 oz fresh white breadcrumbs
    1 small onion
    4 cloves
    ¾ pint milk
    salt and pepper

C

Mix the breadcrumbs with a good pinch of salt, and white pepper. Put them into a fire-proof dish. Peel the onion, leave it whole, stick the cloves firmly into it, and put it in the middle of the dish. Pour hot milk over. Cover, and let it cook slowly in the oven for about an hour. Remove the onion before serving. Serve very hot.

It can be made in a saucepan. Put the onion, stuck with the cloves, into the pan. Add the milk and bring slowly almost to boiling point. Remove from the heat, then stir in the breadcrumbs, mixed with the seasonings. Cover, and leave to infuse for at least $\frac{1}{2}$ hour. Reheat when required, removing the onion and stirring well with a wooden spoon.

A small piece of butter, if liked, can be beaten in just before serving.

For roast chicken, roast turkey, roast pheasant and other game, and good also with sausages.

APPLE SAUCE

    1 lb cooking apples
    1 oz sugar (or to taste)
    $\frac{1}{2}$ oz butter

Peel and core the apples and slice them thinly into an enamel saucepan. Add just enough water to prevent them from catching. Stew them gently, stirring as necessary, until they are soft and cooked down. Beat well with a wooden spoon, adding sugar to taste and a scrap of butter. Reheat when ready to serve.

For roast pork, roast duck and roast goose.

GOOSEBERRY SAUCE

Top and tail and wash the required amount of green goose-berries, say ½ pint. Put them into a pan with the barest amount of cold water and stew them down to a pulp, very gently. Drain off surplus juice. Sieve the cooked fruit, using a nylon strainer or sieve and a wooden spoon. Reheat, with say 2 teaspoonfuls of sugar, or to taste, and a small knob of butter. Serve very hot.

For grilled mackerel.

HORSE-RADISH SAUCE

Horse-radish can be bought ready grated. If using a fresh horse-radish root, wash, scrape and grate it sideways.

    2–3 tablespoonfuls grated horse-radish
    ½ teaspoonful castor sugar
    pinch of salt
    2–3 teaspoonfuls vinegar
    2–3 tablespoonfuls thick cream

Mix all well together, adding a little more cream if wished. Serve cold. It can be kept for a few days in a jar with a tight-fitting lid.

For hot or cold roast beef, also herrings and mackerel.

MINT SAUCE

Spearmint is usual, but some connoisseurs prefer applemint.

Strip fresh leaves of mint from their stalks. Chop the leaves finely or cut into little pieces with scissors. Put them into a sauceboat with 1 teaspoonful of brown sugar to each 2 teaspoonfuls of chopped mint leaves, and pour over them a little very hot water, just enough to cover. Let it cool, then to each initial 2 teaspoonfuls of chopped mint leaves add about 1 tablespoonful of a good vinegar, or according to taste. Let it stand for 2–4 hours before it is served.

Serve with hot roast lamb, with a little good gravy, new potatoes and garden peas. It is either liked very much or not liked at all. Many people prefer lemon juice to the vinegar—it can be diluted a little with water.

A SAUCE FOR BRAWN

Made mustard, brown sugar and brown malt vinegar; mix together just to your taste.

A note on vinegar

Malt vinegar is our customary all-purpose vinegar, but a good wine vinegar is often preferable, for salad dressings especially, and cider vinegar is another alternative.

Note that in country cookery vinegar is often used over-lavishly. Too much vinegar blunts the palate, spoils other flavours and leads to over-dependence on this form of seasoning. A little lemon juice can often be substituted.

5. Fish Dishes

In country districts, unless freshwater fish or supplies from the coast were available, fish was always a luxury. Frozen fish, improved transport, and river and coastal pollution have in their different ways altered the picture; but in any case most country recipe books include very few fish recipes. Favourite economical recipes, most of which are really more 'general' than 'country', tend to fall into three main groups: the fish savouries—fish pies and other made-up fish dishes, sometimes included as Lenten dishes; ways with herrings and mackerel; and the fish stews and soups which are useful for bits and pieces.

Fish savouries

USEFUL FISH MIXTURE

Mix flaked cooked fish (firm white fish or smoked fish) with a good thick white sauce (page 63) made with fish stock and/or milk. Season with salt and pepper. Add grated nutmeg if wished, or, as suitable, grated cheese, made mustard, lemon rind, anchovy essence, chopped parsley, chopped hard-boiled egg, chopped crisp bacon, sliced cooked carrot, cooked mushrooms, picked shrimps or prawns. Heat the mixture up well in the saucepan, and serve on hot buttered toast; or put into greased ramekin dishes or scallop shells, strew with breadcrumbs, dot with butter or margarine, and heat up in a hot oven; or use for fish pies or fish flan (see below).

FISH PIE

A top of browned breadcrumbs is an alternative to the usual mashed potato. Cover the fish mixture with mashed potato or fresh breadcrumbs, dot with butter or margarine, and bake in a hot oven (Mark 6, 400 °F) till hot through and lightly browned, about ½ hour.

FISH FLAN

Make a fish mixture as above, let it get cold, then put it into a flan case or pie plate lined with shortcrust ready to bake. Sprinkle the top with breadcrumbs and dot with butter or margarine; or sprinkle with grated cheese; or decorate with small shapes cut from the remains of the pastry. Bake in a hot oven (Mark 6, 400 °F) for about ½ hour.

FISH CAKES

    8 oz flaked cooked fish
    8 oz mashed potato
    1 oz melted butter or margarine
    salt and pepper
    chopped parsley (optional)
    beaten egg to bind

Mix all the ingredients together, including enough beaten egg to bind them together. Put the mixture on a floured board, shape it into flat cakes, flour them, and fry them in shallow fat. They can be garnished with parsley. Parsley sauce (page 64) or egg sauce (page 64) can be served with them.

FISH BAKE (OR FISH HOT POT)

Bacon and/or tomatoes are usual for this kind of fish savoury. Arrange fillets of uncooked fish, cut in fair-sized pieces, to make a bottom layer in a baking dish. Add a spoonful or two of water. Season with pepper and a little salt if the fish is not smoked. Dot with margarine. Add a layer of sliced tomatoes, then a layer of thin streaky bacon. Cover with a greased paper. Bake in a moderate oven (Mark 5, 375 °F) for about 25 minutes.

Fish with eggs

Uncooked fish in small pieces and eggs broken into the spaces between, with cheese sauce poured on top, can be baked together. Poached eggs often accompany finnan haddock. Some people find such dishes too 'slippery'. A fish soufflé can be the best answer, or flaked cooked fish in scrambled eggs or an omelet.

Herrings and mackerel

No need to dwell on their virtues. For fried herrings with oatmeal see page 124. This method suits mackerel as well.

Mustard sauce (page 67) goes well with either, and gooseberry sauce (page 65) is a traditional sauce for grilled mackerel, cutting the richness.

SOUSED HERRINGS (PICKLED HERRINGS)

Take say 4 fresh herrings, carefully cleaned and filleted. The roes can be retained. Wash the fish well in cold water, sprinkle with salt and pepper, and roll them up from the head end, skin side out. Pack them into a casserole. Add a small raw onion in thin slices (this is not always included), and spices to taste ($\frac{1}{4}$ teaspoonful salt, about 10 peppercorns, 1 or 2 cloves, a small bay leaf, perhaps a blade of mace). Mix about $\frac{1}{4}$ pint each of water and vinegar and pour this over the fish. Brown malt vinegar is usual. Cover, and cook in a slow oven (Mark 1, 275 °F), for 1$\frac{1}{2}$ hours. Leave in the dish to get cold. It should improve if kept for a day (covered when it has cooled) in a cold place. Serve cold from the dish, with salad.

ROES ON TOAST

For herring roes. Use the soft roes. Wash and dry the roes, roll them lightly in flour, cook them gently in butter till golden. This can be done in a saucepan; melt a small knob of butter, and add a little chopped parsley if liked. Serve on hot buttered toast, add pepper; a squeeze of lemon sharpens the flavour.

Kippers

Kippers are usually grilled. They can be dipped in hot water first for a minute, to soften; drain well. Put a dab of butter or margarine on top, grill skin side down, 6–8 minutes.

An old way, instead, was to stand them in a jug of boiling water for 5 minutes or longer, to heat through.

As good a way as any is to poach them in a frying-pan in water barely to cover. Simmer for a few minutes. Drain carefully. Serve with a piece of butter on top.

KIPPER TOAST

Cook the kippers. Remove skin and bones and flake the fish

while it is still hot. Mix well with melted butter or margarine.
Serve spread on toast and well heated under the grill.

Fish stews and soups

These are a very old economical way of using mixed small
amounts of sea and/or freshwater fish. Plaice, skate, dabs, cod,
haddock were often used. Flounders, perch, tench and eels
were a popular mixture for the once-famous Greenwich water
souchy, for which Eliza Acton gives a recipe. For this dish the
fish was stewed gently in salted water to cover, in which a few
sliced parsley roots, with a bunch of green parsley, had first
been simmered until they were tender. It was served with
brown, usually, or white bread and butter.

The following recipe for a fish soup is useful. Any mixture of
suitable fish can be used.

FISH SOUP

    1 lb fish (white fish and/or smoked fish)
       or 1 finnan haddock
    1 or 2 onions
    1 or 2 carrots
    small piece of celery (optional)
    herbs and spices to taste (see below)
    1½ pints water
    1½ oz butter or margarine
    1½ oz flour
    ½ pint milk

Wash the fish. Put it into the pan with chopped onion and
carrot, and chopped celery if included. Add herbs and spices
tied in muslin (perhaps a clove, a few peppercorns, a small bay

leaf, a sprig of parsley). Add salt, depending on whether smoked fish is used. Add the cold water. Bring to the boil, then simmer with the lid on the tilt for about half an hour. Strain. Discard the vegetables. Retain the fish stock. Flake the fish while still hot, removing any skin and bones. Rinse the pan. Melt the butter and stir in the flour, then add the fish stock gradually, stirring well, as for a sauce. Cook and stir for about 5 minutes. Add the milk and the flaked fish, and reheat. Serve very hot, garnished with finely chopped parsley.

6. Meat and Accompaniments

Patterns are changing and various skills and customs have been slipping away, including many that went with pig-keeping, once a major cottage economy. The following are mainly supplementary notes on some of the meat dishes for which recipes are widely available, and also some suggestions for stuffings and other accompaniments.

Lancashire hot pot

If possible, use a straight-sided brown earthenware stew-jar, with 'lugs' ('ears') for lifting. If this is tall enough, the lamb neck chops which are often the choice for the hot pot can be arranged standing on end for easier serving, with sliced potato and onion packed in between, then water added as usual and a roof of potato slices overlapping each other on top. But the hot pot is often assembled in layers. In the following recipe the meat is floured and browned first, which is not always the way.

A SPECIAL LANCASHIRE HOT POT

2 lb lamb chops (best end of neck)
½ lb onions
½ lb carrots
2 lb potatoes (or more)
flour
pepper and salt

dripping (about 2 oz)
bay leaf
thyme and marjoram (optional)
stock or water
1 teaspoonful sugar

Serves about 6 people. Use a large earthenware stew-jar, about 8-pint size. Trim the chops and sprinkle on each side with pepper and flour. Chop the onions. Slice the carrots. Slice the potatoes fairly thickly. Heat some dripping in a frying-pan and fry meat, onions and carrots in turn until lightly browned, removing to the warmed stew-jar. Arrange the chops sloping or standing on end round the sides, with onion and carrot and some of the sliced potato packed into the middle; or arrange in layers. Season with pepper and salt and add the bay leaf and other herbs. Make a good thick layer of overlapping potato slices on top, but before completing it fill up with hot stock or water, stirred round in the frying pan with a little more salt and pepper (but not too much) and a teaspoonful of sugar. The water should come to just below the potatoes on top. Brush the top with melted dripping or butter. Cover with a lid. A sheet of greased greaseproof paper placed under the lid is sometimes a good idea. Remove the lid and raise the oven heat for the last 15 minutes or so for the top potatoes to brown. Put the hot pot into a moderate oven (Mark 4, 350 °F) and give it at least 2½ hours in all.

Irish stew

Traditionally a white stew: potatoes and onions, no carrots, and the meat which was kid originally and then mutton is now usually neck of lamb. A few herbs, thyme especially, improve it, and so can giving it a stir round now and again. By the time the stew is ready the potatoes should be well broken up and cooked down.

Stewed pork

Stewing pork or pork chops can be cooked in layers with sliced potato, plenty of onion, a little sage, and a sliced apple; the apple sharpens the flavour as well as cutting the richness. Add very little water and cook slowly, allowing plenty of time.

Beef stews

Should be rich, brown and well-flavoured. Good flavourings, besides the usual thyme, marjoram, bay leaf and parsley, are a little lemon balm or a strip of lemon rind, a few marigold petals (page 33), two or three cloves stuck into an onion, mushrooms or mushroom ketchup, sometimes instead of water some beer. Jugged steak is stewing steak in small pieces, sometimes floured and slightly browned in some dripping, and sometimes not, *very* gently cooked in a closed jar, with cloves, onion, seasoning, sometimes celery, and no water, and was a favourite substitute for jugged hare. For stewed beef steak and kidney, allow $\frac{1}{4}-\frac{1}{2}$ lb ox kidney to 1 lb of the stewing beef.

Steak and kidney pudding

This is traditionally served in its basin, with a napkin tucked round it, and a jug of plain hot water to accompany—a little is poured into the pudding when cut, and mixed with the rich gravy. Some old recipes include oysters, which used to be cheap. A few mushrooms go well instead.

Steak and kidney pie

Serving hot is usually recommended, but it can be very good cold. Ideally, cook the meat under a rich pastry crust; but with stewing steak it is advisable to cook the meat in advance—then put it into the pie-dish and leave to get cold before adding the pastry and baking for a good ½ hour in a hot oven.

Veal and ham pie

Usually served cold, but can be very good hot, with hard-boiled egg then perhaps better left out. Include bay leaf and a grating of lemon rind.

Meat pasties

Cornish pasty is well known. Best made with raw tender beef steak chopped small, and raw potato and onion chopped very fine. A little finely chopped raw turnip or swede was often included, and a few little pieces of butter dotted about in the filling, to prevent dryness in cooking. Shortcrust pastry is usual, and for each pasty the pastry is now usually cut to the size of a saucer. This pasty originally was a carried meal for a tin-miner, and was eaten cold. Meat pasties were also a favourite standby for farm workers, and might be large or small, often half-moon shaped, sometimes filled with slices of fried or boiled streaky bacon, sometimes with minced meat and grated potato and onion; sliced tomato became quite popular as an addition. They were often eaten mid-morning.

Cottage pie (or shepherd's pie)

Best made with freshly cooked mince and potatoes. When

cooked, the mince and its sauce should be fairly thick. A dash of Worcester sauce or mushroom ketchup is sometimes added. The mashed potato on top should be creamy and buttery, ridged with a fork and dotted with butter or dripping so that it browns up well.

Meat loaf

One of today's main ways of 'stretching the mince', but some of the recipes are inclined to be complicated.

QUICK MEAT LOAF

½ lb minced raw beef
4 oz fresh breadcrumbs
1 egg
seasonings (see below)
dripping or lard

Fork up the mince. Mix it well with the crumbs. Add salt and pepper and other seasonings, such as a pinch of mixed herbs or ground mace, a little chopped fried onion or grated raw onion, perhaps a teaspoonful of ketchup or Worcester sauce. Bind with the beaten egg. Shape the mixture into a loaf with the backs of two spoons. Melt a good knob of dripping or lard in a meat tin. Place the loaf in the tin, using a fish slice, and baste with the hot fat. Bake until brown in a hot oven (Mark 6, 400 °F), for 45 minutes, basting occasionally. Serve hot or cold. If to be served hot, a few parboiled potatoes, cut up, can be roasted round it. Serves 3.

Liver, savoury dishes

Liver makes a good hot pot, with onions and sometimes bacon,

and sometimes tomatoes or apple, or it can be baked with a
forcemeat stuffing—for mock duck, sage and onion—and
streaky bacon.

MOCK DUCK

½ lb calf's liver
sage and onion stuffing (see below)
salt and pepper
3 or 4 rashers streaky bacon
stock or water

Make the stuffing first: see the recipe on page 88, omit egg,
use half quantities. Wash and dry the sliced liver and arrange it
in a greased fire-proof dish. Sprinkle with salt and pepper,
spread the stuffing over, and add a little stock or cold water
barely to cover the liver, then place bacon over the top. Put
a lid on the dish and bake in a very moderate oven (Mark 3,
325 °F) for 1 hour. Remove the lid for the last 15 minutes.

Boiled ham and bacon

Soak in cold water overnight, or as advised. Put into the pan
with fresh cold water to cover. Bring slowly up to the boil,
skim, add flavourings (a little brown sugar, a few peppercorns,
a pinch of mace or one or two cloves, perhaps a bay leaf or a
bunch of sweet herbs, or for a ham a wisp of hay was said to
bring out the flavour). Simmer very gently until tender. Allow
about 25 minutes per pound from when the water has come to
the boil—a little less time for the larger weights, about 25
minutes extra for smaller weights. Leave to set and cool in the
pan for at least ½ hour. Then the rind can be removed and the
surface dressed with browned breadcrumbs.

Meat soups and broths

Usually very substantial, with meat and vegetables cooked together and often barley or oatmeal, sometimes rice, to thicken. Often the soup and the meat are served separately. Scottish recipes are famous, including Scotch broth (neck of mutton or boiling beef, chopped mixed vegetables and pearl barley) and cock-a-leekie (boiling fowl, leeks, sometimes prunes, soaked and added half an hour before serving), both with numerous variations.

All these soups need long simmering. They also need careful skimming if they are not to be greasy, and are therefore sometimes started off a day in advance, as for the Welsh broth below.

WELSH BROTH

Make this with neck of lamb, as much as you need for a main course, and start the evening before. Put the meat in a heavy pan with cold water to cover, add salt, bring to the boil, skim, simmer covered for 1½ hours. Then put it all into a bowl, leave uncovered to cool overnight, and skim off the fat the next day. Allow 2 hours now for cooking time. Start off again in the clean saucepan, returning the meat and skimmed stock, and adding as many kinds as possible of the following vegetables, sliced not too small: 1 onion, 1 or 2 leeks (white parts only, save the green until later), 2 carrots, 1 parsnip if liked, a moderate amount of chopped swede; also 1 oz washed pearl barley. Add more water, to cover. Leave room for potatoes, and add these peeled and halved after the broth has simmered for 1½ hours. Add the chopped green of the leeks then as well. Add chopped parsley shortly before serving. Taste for seasoning. Serve the broth first, as a soup, followed by the meat with most of the vegetables.

Meat reheated

A stew sometimes mellows and improves with reheating—
roast meat, never; if heated up thoroughly it becomes tough
and stringy; if only warmed mildly it lets bacteria flourish, and
food poisoning can be the result. Hash, in its common meaning
of sliced cold meat warmed up in gravy or sauce, is one of the
worst dishes ever invented. Sausage rolls and meat pies, in-
sufficiently cooked or reheated, or both, are also a danger.
Cottage pie, as mentioned above, is better in every respect
when made with freshly cooked meat.

The remains of a stew can be put under a top of potatoes, on
the lines of a 'steam engine'—chopped cooked meat, with
finely chopped onion, extra gravy, and a good close roof of
sliced potatoes; cooked in a moderately hot oven for an hour or
so under a lid, which is then removed for the top to brown. In
this way it can be heated up very thoroughly without drying.

Cold meat

Cold roast or boiled meat cuts well and (see above) is better
cold than reheated. Slow or pot-roasted pork streaky (belly of
pork) is better cold than hot. A whole, cold, boiled chicken or
fowl, coated with a good white sauce made with some of the
chicken stock (or see egg sauce, page 64), and then garnished
with parsley, is excellent for various occasions. Cold meat loaf
is often very good, and goes far. Home-made pork pies used to
be a great speciality. Cold steak and kidney pie, or veal and ham
pie, and cold Cornish pasties, are mentioned above.

Jellied moulds and shapes were very popular in summer, with
salad. They can be made with shin of beef or chicken or
boiling-fowl, all of which are gelatinous and should set well.
Pig's trotters were often used, or a small cow-heel (with

stewing-steak), to give a good set. These are usually bought ready boiled, but need long boiling in any case. Cow-heel is not now very often available, but can sometimes be ordered.

Brawn comes into the above category. Some bought brawns are so tasteless and gluey that a good home-made brawn can be a surprise. Traditionally, brawn comes under pig-cookery and is made with a pig's head (whole or half), pickled, but good small brawns can be made with pig's trotters and jointed chicken. Herbs and spices (peppercorns and cloves, mace or nutmeg) are added to flavour. See page 68 for a sauce. It is best to read a few recipes and then adapt one to suit one's own preferences.

Game birds

Broadly, the season is from August to February. Special dates apply in each case, outside which the bird may not legally be shot, or sold (unless deep frozen).

For the usual ways of preparing and cooking game it is best to refer to detailed basic instructions. When young it is roasted, and when old it is stewed or perhaps put into a pie. Game is hung to tenderize it, and to bring out the game flavour. Game birds are hung (unplucked and undrawn) by the neck. Note that roast game is often preferred well done rather than very rare, and very high game is an acquired taste and not always appreciated.

Hares and rabbits

Hares are in season from the beginning of August to the end of February. Best from October to February. They are classed as game and are hung, usually by the hind legs, for a gamey flavour.

Hares seem to have been looked on by country people with a certain amount of superstition and prejudice. Jugged hare is the best-known recipe, but if given the full treatment it can be quite an extravagant dish and sometimes a trying one to prepare.

Wild rabbits (best from about September to early spring) are not treated as game and unlike hares are gutted straight away. Usually better flavoured than those specially bred. There are many recipes to choose from—bearing in mind that rabbit is inclined to be very dry and needs plenty of herbs to go with it (marjoram is good, and thyme very good), and onion and bacon, and a good sauce or plenty of gravy.

STEWED RABBIT WITH CIDER

  1 rabbit, jointed (weight jointed, about 2 lb)
  flour (about 2 oz)
  salt and pepper
  4 oz streaky bacon
  dripping
  2 onions
  ½ pint cider
  ½ pint water
  bunch of sweet herbs

Wash the joints of rabbit in salted water, dry and coat with flour, seasoned lightly with salt and pepper. Cut up the bacon into fair-sized pieces, fry it lightly and remove to an earthenware casserole. Add a little extra dripping to the bacon fat in the frying-pan and fry the rabbit joints and sliced onion till browned. Transfer to the casserole, mixing well with the bacon, then adding cider and water, a bay leaf and a sprig each of thyme, marjoram, lemon balm, winter savory, or what you will.

Cover the dish. Cook for 2 hours, or a little longer, in a moderate oven (Mark 4, 350 °F). Serves 4.

STEWED WOODPIGEON

The above recipe, for stewed rabbit, also suits woodpigeon. Include a few mushrooms, fried lightly after browning the pigeons, and some good stock can quite well replace the cider.

ACCOMPANIMENTS

To take the edge off the appetite, which they often did very substantially; but above all to add flavour and provide a good contrast, and to counteract dryness or richness.

Suet puddings and dumplings

See the basic suet recipe on page 138. Chopped herbs can be added. This form of 'filler' might either be a big roly-poly (bolster shaped), or, still popular nowadays on occasion, small dumplings cooked with the lid on the pan the whole time so that they will be light. Badly cooked they are heavy and indigestible. A little baking powder is usual.

SMALL DUMPLINGS

For a few small dumplings halve the basic recipe quantities (page 138). Roll into 8 or more dumplings between the floured palms of the hands. Put them into the broth or stew, as it simmers, for the last ¾ hour or so.

Herb puddings

See page 27 for herb puddings made with barley or oatmeal.
These were sometimes eaten with bacon.

Batters

For making the batter for the following recipes see page 99.

YORKSHIRE PUDDING

Traditional with roast beef. It was originally cooked in the tin
that caught the drips from the joint as it roasted above.

Make the batter (page 99). Put 2 or 3 tablespoonfuls of
dripping from the roast to cover the bottom of a meat tin
(about 10 by 7 inches—it must be a tin), and make smoking
hot in the oven. Stir the batter, adding a tablespoonful of very
cold water, pour it into the tin and bake straight away in a hot
or very hot oven (Mark 7–8, 425–450 °F) until golden-brown,
crisp and well risen, 25–30 minutes. It can be made as individual
puddings in fairly deep bun tins or patty pans, 15–20 minutes.

The old Yorkshire way is to serve it, either as individual
puddings or cut into squares, as a separate course with thick
gravy before the meat and vegetables, which were then served
out on to the same plates. The more widespread custom is to
serve the pudding with the meat and vegetables, all together:
it can be served, cut into squares, from a separate dish, or
squares or individual puddings can be placed round the roast.

HERB BATTER (SAVOURY BATTER)

Traditional with roast pork.

Make the batter as for Yorkshire pudding above, stirring in

some chopped cooked onion (one smallish onion is enough), a teaspoonful of chopped parsley, a little sage, thyme, marjoram, chopped, or a pinch of mixed dried herbs, and a dash of pepper. Cook in a tin as above, and serve with the joint.

Stuffings and forcemeats

Both words mean the same. Forcemeat, from the French *farce* (the term 'farce' often occurs in old cookery books), means finely pounded or minced meat used as a stuffing—hence any suitable mixture used either for stuffing or for cooking separately as a garnish. The following are useful examples.

FORCEMEAT FOR A GARNISH

4 oz fresh breadcrumbs
mixed herbs (see below)
2 oz lean ham (optional)
grating of lemon rind (optional)
pinch of ground mace or nutmeg
salt and pepper
1½ oz butter or margarine
1 egg
a little flour
fat for frying

Stir all the dry ingredients lightly round. If ham is included, mince it up very finely. Use either 1 teaspoonful mixed dried herbs, or 2 teaspoonfuls fresh herbs finely chopped. Parsley and lemon thyme, mixed, is a favourite choice. Add the melted butter or margarine and mix well, then add the beaten egg and beat all well together. Flour the palms of your hands and roll into balls about the size of small walnuts. Dust them with flour and fry in hot fat until golden brown. Serve at once to garnish veal, chicken, jugged hare, rabbit. Good in a beef stew. After being fried they can be put into a stew (replace the lid straight away) about 20 minutes before the end of the cooking time.

STUFFING FOR ROAST CHICKEN

2 oz fresh breadcrumbs
2 rashers of streaky bacon (uncooked)
1 teaspoonful chopped fresh thyme and lemon balm
  (mixed)
salt and pepper
1 egg
fresh tarragon, in addition, if possible

Mix together the breadcrumbs and the bacon chopped finely. Add the thyme and lemon balm (about ½ teaspoonful of each). Season lightly with salt and pepper. Bind with the beaten egg. Put in at the neck end of the bird to stuff the breast. If possible put a sprig of fresh tarragon into the body of the bird before roasting, for a very distinctive additional flavour.

For an oatmeal stuffing for a boiling fowl see page 123. 'Sage and onion' is used so often in country cookery that a recipe must be included. Sage offsets richness, but if you don't like it then it can be omitted from the stuffing, which becomes simply onion stuffing instead.

SAGE AND ONION STUFFING

4 fair-sized onions (about 1 lb)
4 oz dry white breadcrumbs

1 teaspoonful powdered sage,
  or 2 teaspoonfuls finely chopped fresh sage
1 teaspoonful salt
pepper
1 oz shredded suet (optional)
1 egg (optional)

Peel and halve the onions and parboil in slightly salted water for 15 minutes, then drain them and chop fairly finely. The crumbs should be dried in a slow oven without letting them colour; this can be done in advance and they can be stored when cool in an airtight jar. Stir breadcrumbs, sage, salt and pepper together. Add the chopped onions. Suet is not always included, and beaten egg not very often, but sometimes both are added when the stuffing mixture is to be cooked separately. Mix all the ingredients well.

For roast pork, duck or goose, or baked liver (see mock duck, page 80). Pork is often roasted plain on the bone, and stuffing served from a separate dish; put the mixture into a greased tin or shallow fire-proof dish and bake until crisp, about 45 minutes.

Big farmhouse bread mixtures, coming under the heading of stuffings, were made with large amounts of stale bread, first soaked in hot water, then squeezed and crumbled and mixed with some milk, with grated onion and/or powdered herbs to flavour. These were baked in a separate tin for an hour or so to serve with roast beef or pork, and gravy.

Some other accompaniments

Gravy, whether as part of a stew or, in the case of a roast, made with the juices and sediment from the dripping, contains

valuable nutriments from the meat. For some traditional sauces
see Chapter 4 (page 63). The jellies classed as 'tart' jellies,
fairly sharp and well flavoured, are good with some of the hot
roasts (especially pork, goose and game) and are sometimes
liked with cold meats as well. Wild fruit jellies are mentioned
on pages 61–2 and 167; they have curious flavours and go well
with game especially. Redcurrant jelly is traditional with roast
leg of mutton, venison and jugged hare. Pickled onions,
pickled walnuts (with cold beef), and pickled red cabbage (with
Lancashire hot pot) must be noted, although nowadays pickles
are usually bought rather than made at home. Good fruits for
chutneys are mentioned on page 59.

7. Eggs

The sight of hens running free is a delight and relief. Every hen has more than a touch of idiosyncracy. In a barnyard, an orchard, a run where they can scratch at the ground and scurry about, they lead lives rich in drama. A good broody hen is wonderfully fierce and obsessive, and becomes the picture of pride when her chicks are streaming around her. The mother hen is a traditional symbol. So is the rooster that heralds the dawn. So, in its mysterious way, is the egg.

Now that so many hens are shut up in batteries or otherwise, real fresh farm eggs are in very short supply. In the past they were often used exceedingly lavishly, but for some families in hard times an egg might well be a luxury, perhaps one a week to keep up the strength of the breadwinner. Eggs are a good source of protein, we know now, and of vitamins also and iron.

Fresh eggs

A fresh egg feels heavy in the hand. As a rule, but depending also on the thickness of the shell, if dropped into cold water an egg should sink if fresh, float if stale and hover on end if in between. The air space in the rounded end expands as the egg becomes older. Evaporation through the pores of the shell makes a vacuum, air then enters to fill it, and with the air the bacteria which can turn the egg bad.

Break a stale egg and the yolk will be flattish and wavery and the white watery.

New-laid eggs

Note well the difference between fresh and very fresh or new laid. Except for very lightly boiled eggs, all eggs for cooking should be not less than 24 hours old, or the whites will not set properly or whip.

To store

Say up to a fortnight in a cool place, if really fresh to start with. Stand with the rounded end (containing the air space) upwards. Keep in a cool and dry place, away from strong light and also away from strong smells, which would be absorbed because egg shells are porous. (Again because of absorption, wipe—do not wash—to clean.) A wooden egg-stand is good. Eggs can be kept in the refrigerator, in a rack, but they go a bit clammy and if taken out and used straight away their shells crack all too easily, yolks tend to break and whites fail to froth up. Remove from the refrigerator or from a cold place about an hour before use, and leave in the warm.

Yolks and whites

The yolk is held by two 'threads'. A fertilized egg (if a cock has run with the hens) contains a dark speck. It will be slightly richer in food value, but will not keep quite so long. Specks and threads can be fished out with a sharp piece of shell.

Yolks and whites can be stored, covered, in the refrigerator or in a very cold place, but do not keep for more than a day or two. Keep yolks separate from whites. Pour a little cold water over unbroken yolks to prevent them from drying.

To separate eggs. The oldest way is the best way. Crack the shell, break in half and tip the yolk from one half to the other, over a basin or cup, until all the white has slipped out.

To whip egg whites. Remember, very fresh (see above) or cold whites don't whip well. There must be no trace of yolk in the white. Use a wide bowl for a whisk, a deep bowl for a beater. A single white can, with an effort, be whipped with a knife or fork on a plate. Utensils must be clean and dry. Beat slowly to start with, then gather momentum, beating continuously until the foam is stiff enough but not grainy. Use soon. Use a metal spoon for lightly folding in sugar (at the last minute) for a meringue, or for folding the whipped egg white into a mixture.

To preserve eggs

This was often a major economy. Country housewives, especially, would put down (preserve) eggs in quantity when they were plentiful. That is, those who had eggs from their own hens to spare, or who could afford to buy extra. The peak time was March and April. Now that supplies and prices are meant to fluctuate less, egg preserving at home has declined, but there has been a slight revival of interest quite recently.

Waterglass. Always the most popular method. Eggs should be clean (if necessary wiped, but not washed), dry, uncracked, infertile (ideally), and fresh (1-3 days old), but not less than 24 hours old. The container can be a zinc pail (or a plastic bucket) or a glazed earthenware crock (the eggs were then sometimes called crocked eggs), and it must be clean and have some sort of lid. Waterglass (isinglass) is sometimes available from an ironmonger's or a chemist's. It has to be mixed with boiled water. Follow the directions exactly. Put the eggs in pointed end downwards. More can be added from time to time. Keep in a cool dry place where the container need not be moved about. The waterglass thickens eventually. Wash the eggs in cold water before use. They should be usable for 9 or 10 months. Break each one separately into a cup, to make sure. They can go into not too delicate pudding and cake mixtures, and can be fried or scrambled, but taste not quite as other eggs and are not good for boiling.

Buttering. This old country way is to rub new-laid eggs, if possible warm from the nest, between the palms of the hands, warmed and well rubbed with butter. (In Ireland these are sometimes called hot-buttered eggs.) The shell should be coated all over. If the eggs are straight from the nest, they will absorb a buttery flavour. They are meant to keep for a month or two. Store, pointed ends down, on egg trays in a cool dry place.

Lard or melted dripping was used in much the same way, to seal the shell thoroughly. Then the eggs should be 24 hours old, so that flavour is not too much absorbed. (As a preservative for the lard, half its weight in borax was mixed with it, and the eggs were meant to keep for say 2 months.) Store as above, on egg trays, or in a container with greaseproof paper tied over, but it should not be airtight, and keep it cool and dry, or the eggs will go musty.

I have never yet tried these methods!

Soft-boiled eggs

Everyone thinks that nobody else can boil an egg properly. My own way is to put the egg(s) into cold water in a pan with no lid, bring to the boil and then boil gently for $3\frac{1}{2}$ minutes. This gives a well-set egg. If the shell breaks in the pan, a few drops of vinegar in the water helps to prevent the egg white from streaming. As soon as the egg is out of the pan, tap it on the top with a spoon to prevent it from hardening. An egg cosy keeps it warm. An old-fashioned horn egg-spoon is the best spoon to use for boiled eggs. They used to be made at the termini of the old drovers' routes and the craft still exists here and there. Stainless steel spoons are good. Silver spoons blacken. The custom of smashing the shell after the egg has all been scooped out is linked to the belief that witches used egg shells to sail in.

Coddled eggs

These are very lightly cooked, but must stand long enough for the whites to be creamy. There is no need for a saucepan. Warm the egg under hot water. Put it into a mug (warmed first, as well), pour boiling water over, cover with a saucer and leave for 12 minutes, but top up meanwhile with more boiling water.

AN EGG IN A CUP

A coddled or lightly boiled egg can be turned out of its shell into a mug or a cup and mixed with little pieces of bread and butter. Children often like eggs in this way.

Hard-boiled eggs

Put the egg(s) into boiling water. Boil for 10 minutes. If boiled for too long, they will smell sulphury when they are shelled. When done, cool unshelled under cold running water and leave in cold water till cold, to prevent a dark line round the yolk.

Here I can't resist putting in Roofs (from *The Gentle Art of Cookery*: see Acknowledgements). 'This is a Lincolnshire dish', says the recipe note. 'The country people made it with the tops of cottage loaves.'

ROOFS

'Two morning rolls, two hard-boiled eggs, one dessertspoonful of anchovy essence; butter and pepper.

'Split the rolls and take out the soft dough inside. Spread both pieces inside liberally with butter.

'Shell and chop the eggs finely; mix them with the anchovy and seasoning, and spread them on both pieces. Put the halves together and bake them till they are very hot and crisp.'

Poached eggs

The eggs must be fresh and good. The best pan to use is a frying-pan. Half fill the pan with water, bring to the boil, let it simmer, add a few drops of vinegar. Break the eggs one at a time into a saucer and slide each one into the water. Draw the white in with a spoon, and spoon the water over the top. Cook gently for 2 or 3 minutes, till set. Lift out with a fish slice, and trim if wished. Serve on thick, hot buttered toast. The toast can be spread with anchovy paste.

POACHED EGGS ON SPINACH

Cook the spinach lightly, drain and press well, add a small piece of butter, season with pepper and salt. Serve with poached eggs on top. A spoonful of cream and/or a dash of nutmeg can be mixed with the spinach. Sometimes cheese sauce (page 64), which must be ready and waiting, is poured over the eggs and browned quickly under the grill.

Scrambled eggs

(1) Break eggs into a basin. Melt a good lump of butter in a

frying-pan. Tip the eggs in. Stir to mix. Add salt and pepper. When the mixture starts flaking, start scraping. Just before it is set, draw the pan from the heat. Eat straight away, perhaps everyone eating straight from the pan as this is a good camp-fire version.

(2) Make hot buttered toast. Break the eggs into a basin, add salt and pepper and 1 tablespoonful of creamy milk for each egg. Beat with a fork to mix well. Melt some butter in a sauce-pan, ½ oz or rather less for each egg. Add the beaten eggs and stir and scrape, over a gentle heat, until almost set. Spoon on to the toast. Serve at once.

Buttered eggs

Beat the eggs and season with salt and pepper. Cook in a buttered basin in a pan of simmering water, beating all the time with a spoon. When almost set, remove from the heat and beat in a good piece of butter, ½ oz to 2 eggs. Eat it very hot, with bread and butter or on hot buttered toast.

Roasted eggs

Prick the rounded end once with a pin. Roast in warm ashes for about 30 minutes, or more prosaically in a very moderate oven (Mark 3, 325 °F) for about 10 minutes less.

Eggs and bacon

For fried eggs and bacon, fry thin rashers of bacon (gammon rashers for ham and eggs), then fry the eggs in the bacon fat, with a scraping of lard or dripping added if necessary. The golden rule is not to have the fat too hot when the eggs go into the pan, and to fry and baste very gently.

D

EGG AND BACON PIE

This old farmhouse standby can be trickier than some of the recipes make it sound. It can be made in an enamel pie plate. For an 8- to 9-inch plate make shortcrust pastry with 8 oz flour, 2 oz lard, 2 oz margarine. Line the plate with pastry, rolled thin. On the pastry spread 3–4 oz thin bacon rashers, cooked very lightly, cooled and cut up a little. Beat up 2 eggs with ½ gill of milk (or a little more milk if it will not overflow). Add pepper and salt. Pour it over the bacon. Cover with a pastry top. Seal well at the edges. Brush over with the remains of the egg mixture to give the pie a rich colour. Do not make the usual hole or slashes to let out the steam, or the filling will boil out; and do not bake in a hot oven, or the pastry will be done before the filling has set. Bake in a moderate oven (Mark 4, 350 °F) for ½ hour.

Omelets

So-called country omelets can be rough and ready, as long as they are fairly substantial. Prepare the 'filling' in advance (chopped cooked ham or bacon, potato, mushrooms, herbs, onion, tomatoes, a mixture of some or all, or what you will). Keep it hot until the omelet is almost cooked, then distribute it on the top. Fold the omelet over, or serve it unfolded.

'One egg' recipes

'One egg for two people' recipes (for egg and bread fritters and small egg and cheese dishes) are worth looking out for, and can be converted to 'Two eggs for two or three people', for slightly more substantial amounts.

One egg can also be used for a batter for Yorkshire pudding (page 86) or pancakes (page 137); sometimes one egg is used in a custard (see below) or for small cakes (page 100).

Batters

Half milk, half water makes the batter lighter. So does a spoonful of cold water added just before use. In winter, country people might add a spoonful of clean dry snow, just before cooking, to lighten a batter.

A USEFUL BATTER

4 oz flour
½ teaspoonful salt (or to taste)
1 egg
¼ pint milk
¼ pint cold water

Sift flour and salt into a bowl. Make a well in the centre, break the egg into the well. Add ¼ pint of the milk and water mixed together, draw the flour from the sides and mix gradually to a smooth paste, then beat till it bubbles. Add the rest of the milk and water, and beat again. The consistency should be like that of thin cream. Put it in a cool place and let it stand for ½–1 hour or so, in the traditional way, but otherwise hurry on and the result will probably work out just as well.

Custards

There are many very old recipes, some of them very rich indeed, for baked custards, 'boiled' custards (but actually custards should be cooked only gently, or the eggs will curdle), and custard tarts.

If flavouring is required, a little vanilla or lemon rind, or a bay leaf, can be infused in the milk, warmed first, for ½ hour.

A USEFUL CUSTARD

1 egg
½ pint milk
2 teaspoonfuls sugar

Beat the egg. For a richer custard use 2 eggs. Heat the milk until hot but not boiling, pour it over the beaten egg, add the sugar, mix well. Rinse the saucepan, pour the mixture into it and cook over a very low heat, stirring all the time and the same way round, until the mixture thickens and coats the back of the spoon. It must not boil. Serve hot, or cold—stir the custard 3 times as it cools.

'The weight of an egg'

One egg and its weight in butter, sugar and flour was in Victorian times, and still is, a favourite mixture for cakes (pages 143 and 158). An average-sized egg weighs just about 2 oz (or say 55 grams).

Bantam eggs

One of these tiny eggs is about half the weight of a hen's egg of average size and can be used (according to weight) in the same ways.

Duck eggs

About twice or one and a half times the weight of a hen's egg.

As ducks tend to lay their eggs in places where they could absorb harmful bacteria, duck eggs should always be very thoroughly cooked. They can be used 1 for 2 hen's eggs for puddings and cakes. They are very enriching.

Easter eggs

Children no longer have much opportunity of hunting for eggs round a farmyard. They can still have an egg hunt at Easter. Hide the eggs, unboiled or hard-boiled, outdoors if possible. They can be left perfectly plain, or marked with the name of the child, or hard-boiled eggs can be dyed in some of the old country ways. The simplest way is to hard boil in water coloured with coffee, tea, cochineal, parsley, spinach, or onion skins (a great favourite). Markings and dyes must be safe if the egg is for eating. A few drops of vinegar in the water gives a sheen.

8. Milk, Cream, Butter and Cheese

MILK

The two main points about milk are that it is a marvellously well-balanced food and that bacteria thrive in it. It contains vitamins, proteins, minerals (calcium, especially), carbohydrates (the milk sugar), and fat (which floats to the surface as cream).

In the past milk was not greatly used for drinking and cooking. That is, not until transport, rapidly, and hygiene, slowly, began to improve during the late nineteenth century. It was used mainly for feeding the calves and for butter and cheese. Skimmed milk was much used for bread-making. Tea, when it began to replace home-brewed beer, was often drunk milkless. In the cottages, fetching the milk sometimes meant a long walk to the farm.

Now that milk is nearly always heat treated, it is necessary to understand (to a certain extent) what this involves, and especially to note the difference between pasteurized and untreated milk and how this affects certain aspects of country cookery.

Pasteurized milk

Nowadays most milk is pasteurized: heated to a temperature below boiling point and then quickly cooled, so as to destroy harmful bacteria, which could be dangerous to health, at the least cost of flavour and food value. Pasteurized milk has a slightly lower vitamin content than untreated milk. It does not sour naturally (see page 105); it simply goes bad. 'Ordinary' pasteurized milk can be set with rennet (page 106) to make junket (page 106) and cottage cheese (page 118).

Pasteurized homogenized milk

The milk, before it is pasteurized, is specially processed so that the globules of fat are broken up into still smaller particles: they remain distributed evenly and do not rise to the surface. In other words it has no 'top of the milk'. It is bland in flavour, very digestible, and no good for junket.

Untreated milk

Raw milk ('farm milk') is at present officially described as untreated milk, with 'farm bottled' added if this is the case. The sale of this grade of milk for household use is now rather rare, and at the moment the future is very uncertain. Raw milk has truer flavour than pasteurized milk, and a very clear cream-line, and it sours naturally (see page 105). Nowadays herds are regularly tested for brucellosis and other diseases, and all farms and dairies where milk is bottled are subject to legal controls, so that raw milk as sold now in this country is usually quite safe to drink, but if in doubt scald it (see below). For young children and babies, as always, get proper advice.

To scald milk

The ordinary household practice is to heat the milk in an uncovered pan almost to boiling point: until it just starts to bubble round the edge. Pour it into a scalded jug (rinsed out with very hot boiled water). Cool quickly, *not* in the refrigerator, but stand the jug in cold water. Scalded milk does not sour naturally (see page 105).

Hot milk

It should be hot, but not boiled. Just scald the milk by heating it as above. If milk is boiled, rather than scalded, it loses food value and can be quite disagreeable.

To wash milk jugs

Rinse in cold water, wash in hot water, final rinse in very hot boiled water (to scald). Put to dry upside down—avoid drying-cloths.

To store milk

Keep covered, preferably in the milk bottle or container, otherwise in a cold clean milk jug. Keep it in the refrigerator or in a cool airy place. Milk left uncovered is easily contaminated and, like other dairy products, tends to absorb smells from food kept nearby. Warmth 'turns' milk. Sunlight destroys some of its goodness and flavour, which is one reason for not letting it stand on the doorstep. Avoid mixing one day's milk with another's.

To keep milk in hot weather without a refrigerator

Even in this day and age this is still useful to know. Stand the bottle or jug in shallow cold water, if possible in a through draught, and covered with a clean damp piece of butter muslin that can trail in the water. The idea is that as the water evaporates, so this cools down the temperature.

Whole milk and separated milk

Whole milk means milk with its full cream content, mixed throughout—generally by shaking the bottle (unless the milk is homogenized) just before opening it, to mix the top of the milk with the rest.

Separated milk, and *skim(med) milk*, mean milk with the cream removed. Although lacking in fat, it is still nutritious.

Sour milk

This section applies to raw milk, unscalded, unpasteurized; see above under untreated milk. Sour is used in the sense of pleasantly acid.

If raw milk is kept in a fairly warm place it will go sour quite soon. This is because raw milk contains lactic acid bacteria (they are present naturally in the milk and are harmless to health), which feed on the lactose (the milk sugar) and convert it into lactic acid—the milk turns slightly sour, and as it gets more sour it thickens. Sour milk, as quite distinct from milk gone bad, is used in many country recipes, Irish and Welsh ones especially, for cakes, bread and scones, usually in conjunction with bicarbonate of soda.

Note. Milk that has been scalded or pasteurized cannot sour naturally. The lactic acid bacteria are destroyed with the other bacteria (page 102).

Curd(s) and whey

The sour milk when thickened can be hung up to drip (page 118) to form a soft curd for cottage cheese and curd cheese cakes. Both are described at the end of this chapter. The thin liquid that remains is the whey. It can be used in baking, instead of fresh milk, for mixing.

Curds can be made from fresh milk by setting with rennet.

Rennet

This rather mysterious agent is used for making milk clot: either raw milk or 'ordinary' pasteurized milk, but not homogenized milk. Rennin is an enzyme in the stomach which has a coagulating action on milk, and rennet is usually prepared from the fourth stomach of a young calf. It is of special importance in cheese-making. Rennet essence for household use is fairly widely available from grocers and chemists. Keep it in a cool dark place and note that it gradually loses strength. Follow the instructions supplied. 1 teaspoonful to 1 pint of fresh milk is the usual allowance. Its main use is for junkets.

Junket

The old name for junket was simply curds—curds and cream when it was served with fresh cream. Junket originally, I understand, was cream cheese made in a rush basket, and what was called Devonshire junket became the junket that we know now. It was made with milk warm from the cow. The creamiest milk is the best for it. It was often flavoured with brandy, especially in the old smuggling days, which must be why it was so very popular in the past. A grating of nutmeg on top is also a traditional flavouring. Coloured flavourings don't really suit it. It can be made either sweet or unsweetened, then served with sugar if wished and/or whipped cream—sometimes lightly spread over it, with nutmeg grated on top—or clotted cream as was the custom in Devonshire. Stewed fruit, not too acid or watery, can accompany.

A DEVONSHIRE JUNKET

1 pint fresh milk
1 teaspoonful rennet essence
1 dessertspoonful castor sugar
1 dessertspoonful brandy
whipped or clotted cream

Heat the milk just to blood heat (test with little finger). Pour into a glass or china dish. Add brandy and sugar. Add the rennet, stir gently, see that sugar dissolves. Leave in a moderately warm place until it sets (allow up to 2 hours or so) and do not move the dish until then. Serve with thick cream.

If the junket is moved before it has set, it will break up into curds and whey. Once it has set, it can be moved to a cool place or the refrigerator. For separate small junkets, mix in a jug then pour into small dishes or glasses to set.

Beestings (various spellings)

This is the first milk from a cow after calving. Actually the second milking is generally preferred. Those who have the chance of using it will probably know very well how to do so. Gifts of it were made ceremoniously. It is very rich, and is much prized for Yorkshire puddings (1 teacupful to equal 2 eggs), rich custards and various old traditional delicacies. There are some of these recipes in *Farmhouse Fare* (see Acknowledgements).

Buttermilk

The liquid resulting from butter-making. The cream turns into butter and buttermilk. Fresh buttermilk is much praised as a drink, but nowadays most of the buttermilk is used for industrial purposes. Cultured buttermilk is sometimes obtainable, but not very widely. In cookery, buttermilk is used like sour milk (page 105), mainly for scones and soda bread.

CREAM

In the old days the milk was left to stand in a setting-pan in the cool of the dairy. The cream rose to the top and was skimmed off with a skimmer, also known as a fleeter, a metal scoop with holes for letting the milk run through. Eventually, setting-pans were replaced by the mechanical separator, which whirls milk and cream apart. Today, most cream is heat treated, to destroy harmful bacteria, and is mass produced at large centres.

Single and double cream

Today, fresh cream is nearly always sold pasteurized. Single cream is thin cream for pouring. It will not whip. Double cream, compared with single cream, contains more than twice as much butterfat. It will start turning to butter if whipped for too long—take care.

Clotted cream

A speciality of the West Country, and well known also as either Cornish or Devonshire cream. The 'clotting' results from a special scalding process (the old method was over a wood fire), which makes it crusty and crumbly. It is very delicious for a cream tea with scones or in Cornish or Devonshire splits (split tea-buns), with strawberry jam.

Sweet cream and ripened cream

Sweet cream means fresh cream. Ripened cream means just slightly soured cream, which thus has more flavour.

These terms are used chiefly in connection with butter-making (page 110). Usually nowadays cream is soured by adding a culture. Pasteurized cream will not sour naturally (page 105).

To whip cream

Keep everything cold. An egg-beater, used slowly to start with, gives good results. Stop before it's too late.

To store cream

Keep it cool, tightly covered, preferably in a refrigerator—then the usual advice is not for more than 2–3 days in summer, 3–4 days in winter. Remove from the refrigerator a little while before serving, to bring out the flavour. As a rule, most cream thickens with keeping.

Country ways with cream

Far removed from rich 'gateaux' and gourmet sauces, most country ways with cream are very simple and subtle: fresh mushrooms cooked gently in cream in a shallow dish; a little cream and nutmeg added to finely chopped spinach; thick cream mixed with mashed turnips; cream cheese (page 118); strawberries or raspberries and cream; whipped cream for fruit fools or with fruit pies, summer pudding (page 134), hot ginger-bread, and with scones and jam for cream teas; cream with the porridge for breakfast. For blackcurrant leaf cream see page 28.

BUTTER

The main use of cream is for butter-making. Briefly, the traditional sequence is separating and ripening the cream, churning, draining (to drain out the buttermilk), washing and salting. In the past, where country butter was made in a small way it might seldom be eaten at home, but taken perhaps long miles to market. In this age of bulk manufacture, home-produced butter is outweighed by imported, and real farm butter is rare.

Farm butter

Much more individual in flavour than manufactured butter. Does not keep quite as long.

Note that butter made from ripened cream has more flavour than that made from sweet cream, as most of our butter is now (page 109).

Fresh butter

This means unsalted butter. It does not keep as long as the salted (but keeps well if deep frozen). It was favoured for best bread and butter for tea-time.

Clarified butter

In country cookery clarified butter is used chiefly for sealing potted meat, game and fish.

To clarify butter: Melt the butter very gently in a small very clean saucepan, skim, let it stand off the heat until the sediment has sunk to the bottom, and then in the ordinary way just pour off the clear 'oil', leaving the sediment behind in the pan, or else strain it off through a muslin or a very fine strainer.

It is sometimes called oiled butter or melted butter.

'Melted butter'

In family recipes this can have one of three meanings: either just what it says, as for instance when a knob of butter is melted round in a pan for vegetables to be tossed in it; or in the special sense of 'oiled' or clarified butter (see above); or, thirdly, as a very frequent abbreviation for melted butter sauce (page 63).

To soften butter

Put the butter into a warm, dry bowl, cut it up, beat smooth with a wooden spoon.

To 'bulk' butter

A homely way of making butter go further for spreading is to mix it with a little warm milk or water (2 or 3 tablespoonfuls to 4 oz butter), beating well. Use straight away.

Butter quantities

When the cooking was done by rule of thumb, a knob of butter was often described as 'the size of an egg' (about either 1 or 2 oz), or 'the size of a walnut' (1 oz); just a 'nut' usually meant about ½ oz and so probably did a 'gooseberry', and then there was 'the size of an acorn'. A little more or less should not make too much difference.

To keep butter

To store, keep it wrapped. As with other fats, light and air cause rancidity. Also, fats easily absorb other flavours. Keep it in a refrigerator preferably, or in a cool, well-ventilated place. Keep unwrapped butter in a covered dish. Glass, china, glazed earthenware are cooler than plastic and less inclined to take on a 'taint'. The earthenware 'butter-cooler' is now a thing of the past. In hot weather, if there is no refrigerator, put the butter in a covered earthenware dish; stand this in a dish of cold water. Some say a spoonful of salt in the water. Cover with butter muslin or similar and let the ends trail in the water, as for milk in hot weather (page 104).

Good uses of butter

Prices have risen, and in any case there has always been a chorus of warnings against too rich a diet. However, butter is sustaining, appetizing and an important source of vitamin D, and some of its uses are quite unsurpassable.

Cakes made with butter are moist and keep well, and pastry is short. It gives a fine flavour to both. For pastry it is usually combined with lard, half and half. It is essential for shortbread, both for flavour and texture. If used instead of margarine for a fruit crumble, it makes all the difference.

Other main uses are for shallow frying fresh fish; for bringing out the flavour of vegetables (spinach and mushrooms especially); and for omelets and scrambled eggs. See page 25 for herb butters.

Butter and other fats

Margarine in place of butter is satisfactory for most general purposes, but for frying and tossing it is inclined to stick. Avoid it for greasing cake tins. Besides spreading well, it creams well for cake and pudding mixtures. Half lard, half margarine makes a good pastry.

Lard besides being useful for frying and pastry making, and foremost for hot water crust for pork pies, is often used in country cake recipes, generally with spices and/or dried fruit to counterbalance the flavour. In cottages home-rendered lard was often used instead of butter for spreading on bread, and was much loved flavoured with rosemary.

Dripping, in country cookery, is used often for frying and browning; also, usually clarified, for rather solid cakes such as soda cake. Keep different kinds separate in small covered dishes. There is seldom much of one kind or another to go into a basin, but small trimmings of fat from meat can be rendered down, and fat from fried bacon has many uses. Good beef dripping is used for bread and dripping, and hot dripping toast.

To clarify dripping: Put it into a saucepan with an equal amount of cold water, bring to the boil, leave till cold, then lift out the fat and scrape any sediment off the underside. For keeping, or if to be used for frying, reheat the fat in a clean saucepan until it stops bubbling, let it cool a little and strain it into a jar.

Oil is the best fat for deep frying, because it can be heated high without burning. If unclarified butter is used for shallow frying, a little oil can be added so that it burns less easily.

Country customs and recipes often more than amply reflect the importance of fat in the diet to keep people warm, and to keep them going, especially in cold weather, and on long walks, and through long heavy outdoor activity.

CHEESE

Cheese has much the same nutritional value as milk, but in compressed form, and 2 oz of cheese is generally said to 'equal' 4 oz of meat. Its advantages as a convenient, well-flavoured, high-protein food have been specially important in country life, and to miners and mill workers, and have become still more widely important in present times.

The traditional farmhouse cheese depends on the cows and their pasture, the time of year and the climate, the particular skills and methods employed, and the length of maturing— with most distinctive and subtle results (though there used to be some dreadful results, hard as nails, from skim milk from the butter-making). Today cheese is made at only a few farms. Most of our main surviving regional cheeses are now mass produced, but often to a high standard. Descriptions of their characteristics are published quite widely. The following notes give reminders.

Regional cheeses

Caerphilly. Semi-hard, quick to ripen. White, mild, slightly salty, refreshing. Still regarded as a Welsh cheese, though now made mainly in Somerset.

Cheddar. Close-textured, pale golden, nutty-tasting. Excellent all-purpose cheese, especially when well matured. Grates well when dry. Young Cheddar: firm and mild. Mature Cheddar: stronger in flavour, richer in colour, slightly crumbly in texture.

Cheshire. Said to be our oldest of cheeses. Three versions: red (dyed), white (creamy) and blue (rare). Crumbly, salty, robust. Toasts and melts very well.

Derby. Close, moist, white, sometimes honey-coloured, fresh-tasting, variable. Layers of chopped sage leaves go into marbled green Derby sage cheese, a Christmas delicacy.

Dunlop. An Ayrshire cheese. Creamy colour. Very mild when young. When it matures, the flavour is rather like that of young Cheddar.

Double Gloucester. Golden colouring usually. When ripe, pronounced subtle flavour. Goes well with stewed apricots.

Lancashire. Spreads and crumbles easily. Creamy-white. Famous for toasting, known as 'Old Toaster'. Young Lancashire: mild and sharp. Matured: very strong.

Leicester. Mild, flaky, carrot-coloured (carrots were originally used for the colouring), melts well.

Wensleydale. Originally made by the monks of Jervaulx Abbey in Wensleydale, and then by the local farmers' wives. Blue Wensleydale rare now. White Wensleydale usual. Creamy, flaky, delicate, honeyed. The best cheese with apple pie.

Stilton. Blue Stilton: blue-green veined, slightly golden, rich and full-flavoured, a fine cheese for Christmas. White Stilton: mild, fresh-tasting, crumbly.

Note. There are some excellent traditional Scottish soft cheeses.

Cheese uncooked

The traditional 'ploughman's lunch' of bread and cheese and raw or pickled onion has now become fashionable. The bread should be wholemeal for preference. Oatcakes go well with cheese and are light but sustaining. Cheese needs balancing and apart from the onions, celery is good with it, and raw apple. Watercress goes very well. Cheese and tomatoes are popular for a sandwich, but the two textures together can be rather too slippery. Fresh, not too finely chopped parsley is a better alternative. In the north it is customary to serve cheese with the apple pie. 'A piece of pie without the cheese is like a hug without the squeeze'—according to one of the sayings. It is also eaten with mince pies and fruit bread, and goes well with gingerbread. In the 'stiff south' it is customary to be shocked by such ways.

To cook cheese

The golden rule is to melt it. If over-cooked it is stringy and indigestible, and often blamed for bad dreams. For cheese sauce (page 64), stir it in at the last over a gentle heat. For toasted cheese, heat it gradually and not for too long. For browned cheese dishes such as cauliflower cheese (page 40), grate it and brown it quickly.

All kinds of cheese 'savouries' made comforting supper dishes in the past: Welsh rabbit, Scotch woodcock, cheese pudding, cheese pasties, cheese and onion dishes, and many other cheese and vegetable dishes.

CHEESE AND ONION PIE

shortcrust pastry made with 6 oz flour, 1½ oz lard,
   1½ oz margarine
8 oz sliced onion
salt and pepper
2 oz grated cheese
2 tablespoonfuls milk
½ oz butter

Line an 8-inch pie plate with half the pastry, rolled thin. Boil thin slices of onion in not too much water until they are soft, drain well, let them cool, then put them on to the pastry, add salt and pepper and sprinkle with grated cheese. Add the 2 spoonfuls of milk, dot with butter. Cover with the rest of the pastry, sealing the edges. Make 2 small slits in the top to let out the steam, and brush it over with milk. Bake in a moderately hot oven (Mark 5, 375 °F) for about 25 minutes, until the pastry is cooked and golden. Serve hot or cold.

CHEESE AND BAKED POTATOES

Bake potatoes in their jackets. When they are ready, split each one nearly in half and fill the gap with a piece of cheese that melts well. Put back in the oven at a low heat (Mark 2, 300 °F) for about 10 minutes, until the cheese has just melted. These potatoes are good to serve with cold ham.

Grated cheese

Dry, hard, well-matured cheese is the best for grating. To harden it up if too soft, hang it in a muslin bag, or wrap loosely in greaseproof paper and keep for a little while, watching well, in the refrigerator. Grated cheese keeps well in a covered jar in the refrigerator or, if tightly covered and very dry, in a cool place.

To store cheese

Not always easy. Air and cold dry it, warmth and damp make it sweaty or mouldy. Best to buy it in good condition and use it up soon. Wrap cut cheese in greaseproof paper or clingwrap and keep it in the bottom of the refrigerator, or in a cool place.

Watch it well. Change wrapping if necessary. Remove from refrigerator well before eating, ½–1 hour, to bring out the flavour.

Cottage cheese

For sour milk, curds and whey, and the use of rennet see
pages 105–6.

Cottage cheese is the old country way of using up sour or
surplus milk, and was generally made at the end of the day.

If raw milk (page 103) has just started to sour, put it in a
warm place to thicken, or heat very gently over hot water.
Then salt it slightly, about ¼ teaspoonful salt to 1 pint of milk,
stirring well. Pour it on to a piece of scalded cheesecloth or
butter muslin (this can be draped over a strainer resting on top
of a basin), tie it up and hang it over a basin to drip. Leave
overnight, or for 24 hours. Sour milk that has gone thick can
be hung up to drip straight away. Curds made from fresh milk,
either raw or pasteurized, can be used. Set the milk with rennet:
1 teaspoonful rennet essence to 1 pint of milk, or as directed—
then hang up to drip as above. It will lack the light acid flavour,
but is useful for cheese cakes (see below).

When most of the whey has drained out, press between two
plates and then scrape the firmed curd from the cloth. Put it
into a bowl, add a little more salt if wished, and mix well, with
a fork. A little cream can be worked in, if available. Finely
chopped chives or parsley can be added to flavour. Use soon.

This is the usual way for home-made cottage cheese. Sometimes, though, it is called curd cheese or cream cheese. Com-
mercially, cottage cheese is made from fat-free (separated) milk,
and curd cheese from the whole milk. Cream cheese, made with
milk and/or cream, is not now often home made. A beautiful
way of serving cream cheese was to put it on hazel leaves.

Cheese cakes

Originally an old farmhouse delicacy for harvest, sheep-shearing and other feasts and special occasions. Many variations —including, as time went on, some far departures from the true theme.

To make them in the old way, make cottage cheese (see above). The curd is now usually set with rennet. To the firmed curd from 1 pint of milk, or to about ½ lb bought *curd* cheese, add a little soft butter (1–2 oz), a little sugar, a beaten egg or 2 yolks, a few currants if wished, perhaps a few drops of brandy or rum, and if wished a grating of lemon rind and/or nutmeg. Sometimes the nutmeg is grated on top before baking. Beat all well together. Line greased patty pans, or a sandwich tin, with good shortcrust pastry rolled thin, made with 4–6 oz flour. Fill half to three-quarters full with the mixture. Bake until golden brown in a hot oven (Mark 6, 400 °F), for 25 minutes or so, depending on size of tin. Eat hot or cold. Ideally they were kept in the cool of the dairy.

9. Oatmeal

Oatmeal builds strength and stamina. In Scotland it was a staple food, and in parts of the north of England as well, where men who strode the hills were said to be 'all legs and wings'.

Many different uses were handed down in the regions where porridge and oatcakes, in one form or another, were a major part of the diet. Some are still well known; others are almost forgotten. The dales havercakes, for example—last I think met with only in Wensleydale—were made by the farmers' wives with great expertise, 'thin as a sixpence and as large as a dinner plate', in dozens so that there was a good stock of them laid in for hay-time. Like most good oatcakes, they were light and crisp, but sustaining; kept and carried well, and went well with light cheese, which for a long day's work is also just right.

Bannocks also were rather like oatcakes. They were made (with stone-ground barley or oats) on a bakestone until the use of the girdle or griddle (in Ribblesdale the oatcakes were called riddle bread).

Oatcakes

Today, though usually bought, they are either cooked on a girdle or baked in the oven. It still takes skill to make them successfully. They can be thick or thin. The two most detailed recipes I have are from Ireland.

THIN OATCAKE

½ lb fine oatmeal
½ teaspoonful salt
pinch of bicarbonate of soda
1–2 teaspoonfuls lard, or fat from fried bacon
¼ pint (about) of boiling water

Add salt and soda to meal; dissolve fat in the water, add the hot water to the meal to make a stiff paste. Flatten with the hand and roll out quickly to the thickness of a sixpence (i.e. as thinly as possible) on a board sprinkled with plenty of oatmeal. Cut in rounds with a saucepan lid, then across in quarters. Place on a fairly hot greased girdle; cook on one side till the corners begin to curl, then turn carefully and cook until dried through, but not brown. They are often toasted on the second side, before a hot fire (or in a hot oven). Keep in a tin box. When wanted, put in the oven for a few minutes to freshen them.

To test the girdle: Hold the flat of the hand ½ inch above it before it gets too hot. If the heat is comfortable, the girdle is fairly or moderately hot.

THICK OATCAKE

½ lb fine oatmeal
2 oz margarine or lard
½ teaspoonful salt
¼ pint (about) cold water
¼ teaspoonful bicarbonate of soda

Add salt and soda to meal, rub the fat into the meal, mix to a stiff paste with cold water. Flatten with hand, on a board sprinkled with oatmeal, to ½ inch thick. Cut into 8 scones; cook on a greased tin in a moderate oven for ½–¾ hour, or until quite dried through.

For most baking purposes oatmeal is usually mixed with some flour.

OATMEAL SCONES

4 oz flour
4 oz oatmeal (fine or medium)
2 oz margarine
¼ pint milk
good pinch of salt
1 teaspoonful baking powder

Mix dry ingredients together, rub in the fat, mix to a soft dough with the milk. Divide the dough into 2. Knead lightly on floured board and shape quickly and lightly into 2 rounds, about ½ inch thick, then cut them in quarters. (Alternatively, roll out the dough ½ inch thick and cut out into round scones.) The tops can be brushed with milk. Bake on a greased baking-tray in a hot oven (Mark 7, 425 °F), for about 15 minutes.

Parkins

These usually have oatmeal included and are among the best of the gingerbread recipes. They can be baked in a meat tin. The oven should be on the slow side. Good recipes, chiefly for Yorkshire parkin, are widespread. In Yorkshire it is the custom to make it for Bonfire Night (5 November). Best made a week or two in advance and stored in an airtight tin—sometimes a small pippin was put in the tin to keep the parkin from going too dry.

Oatmeal stuffing

In the Scottish tradition. Excellent for a boiling fowl. The bird, trussed for boiling, has some of the stuffing put into the neck end and some of it into the body, with space left for the stuffing to swell, and the tail end is then sewn up securely with thread. Some lemon juice is squeezed over the breast and the fowl is wrapped in greaseproof paper and tied with string, then simmered gently with carrot, onion and seasonings (salt and pepper, a clove or two, a bay leaf), in the usual way, and served hot or cold with a sauce. The sauce is made with stock from the pan, and some milk (see also egg sauce, page 64). The stuffing gives a good, subtle flavour.

OATMEAL STUFFING FOR A FOWL

4 oz medium oatmeal
2 oz shredded suet
1 small onion
salt and pepper

Mix the oatmeal, suet and onion until they bind well together. The onion should be parboiled first and chopped finely. Season very carefully with salt and pepper.

Oatmeal savoury dishes

Skirlie is oatmeal fried in hot dripping with a small amount of finely chopped, lightly fried onion. There are some rather debatable scrapple recipes, when a sort of meat loaf is made with oatmeal and pork, or pork sausagemeat; then left to cool, and then sliced and fried. Oatmeal pudding (a savoury boiled or steamed pudding, to eat with a little meat or thick gravy) is very substantial. Double the quantities in the stuffing recipe

above, add a little cold water to mix and ¼ teaspoonful bicarbonate of soda, steam in a greased basin in the usual way for
steamed puddings for 1½–2 hours. Of the savoury recipes, the
following is now perhaps the best known, and it is the best way
of cooking fresh herrings.

FRIED HERRINGS IN OATMEAL

The herrings should be well cleaned, with the heads and fins
removed. They have an extra fine flavour if fried unsplit 'on
the bone'. For quicker cooking and eating, split and bone,
easing the backbone away. Dry the herrings well. Allow about
½ oz (about a tablespoonful) of coarse or medium oatmeal for
each, season the oatmeal with salt and pepper, and toss each
fish separately in it to coat well. Fry in hot dripping or butter,
quite slowly, until golden brown on both sides. Serve on very
hot plates. A little vinegar can be sprinkled over if liked, or
serve with mustard sauce (page 65).

Porridge

Very few collections of recipes give a traditional porridge
recipe, for a hot breakfast.

OATMEAL PORRIDGE

Per person:
½ pint water
1 handful (1–1½ oz) oatmeal (coarse or medium)
¼ teaspoonful salt

But proportions should be according to taste. Use a strong pan
or a double boiler. Bring the required amount of water to the
boil. Trickle in the meal with the left hand, little by little (this

was the old way), and stir all the time with the right hand, using a wooden spoon. Stir until it thickens (about 5 minutes). When all is well mixed and not 'claggary' (I have never seen this word, which speaks for itself, written down), cover the pan and cook very gently for about ½ hour, stirring now and again. If using a double boiler, allow say ½ hour longer.

Rolled oats

Often chosen for porridge because, being heat treated, they cook quickly. The porridge can be improved by cooking for a little longer than stated in the usual instructions; if using a double boiler, cook longer still.

Also useful for flapjacks and the kind of baked fruit pudding that is sometimes just called a 'bake'.

To buy and store oatmeal

Grindings vary from fine to coarse. Nowadays, medium oatmeal is the kind most often available, and answers for most purposes. Oatmeal is quite rich in fat. It does not keep very well, unless cooked, and quite easily goes mouldy or bitter, or loses aroma. Buy it in to use soon, and store a fresh lot each time (not a fresh supply in with the last lot). Keep it in a dry place, in an airtight container. A tin is best, with a good lid.

10. Honey, Treacle and Sugar

HONEY

Modern methods of bee-keeping originated in the mid-nineteenth century. The association of honey with almost magical properties goes right back through the ages. The word 'magical' comes very readily. Some of the components of honey are still a mystery, in spite of scientific research. As well as sweetening, it is antiseptic, soothing and healing, and moisture-retaining; hence its renown as a natural cosmetic, in ancient times as well as today. Also, because most of the sugar in honey has been 'broken down' by the bees (sucrose is inverted into glucose and fructose) and is quickly taken into the bloodstream, honey is specially digestible and energy-giving. It is often recommended for invalid diets, and for children. It is well known as an 'instant reviver'—besides being much used for cold cures and nightcaps and to sweeten herb teas (see the chapter on Drinks and Remedies). Best used unheated, or warmed only gently, but not heated to a high temperature. Keeping qualities are exceptional, if it is stored under normal conditions; it will not ferment or go mouldy.

Flavour and texture

True honey is produced by the bees from nectar. Nowadays, bees are often heavily fed on sugar and then the honey is not what it should be. The rate of granulation depends on the particular nectars in the honey and their proportions, and ways in which the honey is treated.

Set honey (granulated), thick in texture, is firmer for spreading. If honey has gone too stiff, stand the jar in almost boiling water, or put it in a warm place.

Clear honey (strained, light, liquid, thin, runny or run honey) is lighter for pouring and blending.

Local honey: a true local honey is prized for its particular flavour—of fruit blossom, clover, gorse, heather, according to the main source of nectar. Clover honey is light in colour and flavour. Heather honey is 'peaty' and strong, and quite different.

Blended honey (different kinds mixed) is less costly, very varied in quality, and is sold very widely.

Honeycomb is now a rare luxury, but sometimes 'chunk' honey is sold, liquid honey with a piece of the comb put into the jar.

Uses of honey in cookery

All over the country, honey was the common method of sweetening until sugar took over. It is now more expensive than sugar. It is important to make the best use of it. Some of the honey recipes of the past, and quite recent ones, are very extravagant unless there is honey to spare. Some of them—especially the honey 'creams' and 'dessert' recipes—are too sweet and cloying for everyone's taste.

Many of the best ways with honey are when it is eaten plain and uncooked: with hot scones (plain, oatmeal or wholemeal), on breakfast toast or hot buttered toast (honey sandwiches are made mainly for children, but some children find them too sweet), with pancakes, oatcakes, hot porridge.

Honey goes excellently with nuts and with fresh or dried fruit.

FRUIT SALAD WITH HONEY AND NUTS

Take a mixture of fruit of your choice. Put it into a dish. Then take some clear honey, warm it slightly, and run it over the fruit. Sprinkle chopped nuts on top.

BAKED APPLES WITH DRIED FRUIT AND HONEY

Choose fair-sized apples, one for each person. Wash them well. Prick the skins here and there with a fork, remove the core with an apple-corer. Place in a not-too-large tin or oven-dish, and fill the centres with dried fruit mixed with honey. Then pour a little water into the dish and bake in a moderate to fairly hot oven (Mark 4–5, 350–375 °F) until the apples are cooked. Times vary, but say about 45 minutes. Eat with a little more honey if wished.

Honey for cakes and jam-making

For those who wish to use honey with or instead of sugar for baking or jam-making, there are certain points to remember:

Honey burns easily.

The use of honey in jam-making quite alters the flavour of jam or marmalade, and can give too soft a set. Half sugar, half honey is one suggestion; or, for a firmer result, three-quarters the amount of sugar to one quarter of honey; but I have not tried either.

Cakes with honey in them keep well (because it is moisture-retaining). Honey can be used for cake-making in the same way as syrup and treacle, but without experience it is a bit tricky to substitute honey for sugar in cake recipes (the amount of liquid, and the method, also come into the question). It is usually simpler to use a honey recipe in the first place and to follow it closely.

Honey is good in tea-bread recipes, where just a little sweetening is needed; it is often the custom to include some chopped nuts as well.

HONEY NUT LOAF

4 oz wholemeal flour
4 oz plain flour
1 teaspoonful baking powder
¼ pint milk
3 oz margarine
1 oz chopped nuts
2 tablespoonfuls honey

Rub the fat into the flour sifted with a pinch of salt and the baking powder. Warm the honey and milk together over a slow heat, then mix them in, and add the chopped nuts. Turn the mixture into a small loaf tin well greased and floured. Bake in a moderate oven (Mark 4, 350 °F) for about 45 minutes.

SYRUP AND TREACLE

Like honey, syrup and treacle give cakes a closer and moister texture and stronger flavour. Used in many traditional cake recipes, especially parkins and gingerbreads, and for tea-breads and scones. Also in puddings and pastry dishes, and golden syrup can be used to sweeten and flavour stewed fruit. Treacle, darker than syrup and much stronger flavoured, is held to be

E

a good source of iron. It is often referred to as black treacle, and syrup as golden syrup. In some recipes the two are combined to give a medium-strong flavour (see half and half gingerbread, page 156). On the other hand, golden syrup is sometimes simply called treacle. It is golden syrup that is generally used for a treacle tart; for a version that is not quite so sweet, the syrup can be mixed with some marmalade.

TREACLE AND MARMALADE TART

shortcrust pastry made with 6 oz flour,
 1½ oz lard, 1½ oz butter or margarine
1½ oz fairly dry breadcrumbs
6 oz golden syrup
2 tablespoonfuls orange marmalade

Line an 8-inch pie plate with shortcrust, building up a good rim. Fill with a layer of breadcrumbs and the syrup slightly warmed and mixed with the marmalade—ordinary breakfast variety. Sprinkle with any remaining crumbs. Cut strips from the pastry trimming to make a lattice top. Bake for ½ hour in a hot oven (Mark 6, 400 °F). Serve warm or cold.

Extra marmalade can be substituted for some of the syrup.

SUGAR

Sugar, arriving from the West Indies, became more plentiful in this country during the eighteenth century, and its consumption shot up by leaps and bounds. In the cottages it was mainly stirred gratefully round in innumerable cups of tea. The general habit of tea-drinking encouraged a taste for cakes, jam and sweet pastries. In the nineteenth century the 'pudding course' came into its own. After the rising obsession for sweetness at all costs, the tendency nowadays is to cut down on sugar, for the sake of good health and good teeth, apart from the fact that prices have risen. When recipes for 'sweets' and puddings are used, or for sweetening fruit, the amount of sugar can often quite easily be reduced. Alterations to cake recipes need more care.

Brown sugars (but sometimes now they are dyed—their quality varies considerably) are used a great deal in country cookery to give cakes and puddings a good rich colour and flavour. Demerara sugar, often used for sweetening fruit, is sometimes said to be too coarse for cake-making, but if well blended into the mixture it is usually very good. When moist sugar is specified, usually for dark fruit cakes and gingerbreads, this means a soft, sticky brown sugar.

For sugar in fruit cookery see page 57, and in jam-making page 162.

11. Puddings

Now for the question of puddings, bearing in mind the words on sugar in the last chapter, and the fact that until much cheaper sugar began changing the pattern most of our ancestors ate very few puddings (the sweet kind)—very few sweet things at all. When packets and tins began to appear on the scene, the changes were carried still further. Farmhouse 'dainty taste' soon developed, with dependence on custard powder, packet blancmanges, condensed milk and tinned fruit. Today, to a certain extent, there is a reaction against over-sweetness. There is less emphasis on the 'sweet course', but when occasion arises some of the simpler old-fashioned recipes are favoured, fruit puddings and fruit pies especially.

Fruit tarts and pies

The terms are somewhat interchangeable. Fruit tarts, hence their name, were originally baked without sugar, so that the juice did not run too much and make them difficult to man-oeuvre, especially when cooked on the girdle.

For general instructions, see any good general cookery book, and special recipes are abundant. Ordinary shortcrust pastry suits most country recipes. A plate pie (plate tart), now usually baked on an enamel or fire-proof glass pie plate, is a favourite version. A mincemeat plate pie or latticed tart is a useful alternative to the usual small 'individual' mince pies. Sometimes the pastry covering of a tart was cut out to leave it open on top, with a border of pastry about an inch wide, and it was then finished with thick rich custard and/or thick cream. There are also numerous versions of meringue tops, including spreading the pastry covering, after baking, with beaten egg white, sprinkling with sugar and returning the tart to the oven for the 'icing' to crisp. This last is the finish for a Cumberland cake, served hot, for which a pastry-lined pie plate is filled with mixed dried fruit plus a little butter and sugar—an example of a tart called a 'cake'.

Favourite fruits for pies and tarts are gooseberries, sometimes for Whitsuntide; cherries (morello are recommended for cooking); a few extra cherries can be stewed separately, with some sugar, and their juice thickened slightly with arrowroot and poured, boiled up, into the pie while it is still hot from the oven, through a pie funnel; plums; rhubarb; apricots, which apparently flourished in England, and were much more common than they are now, until about the mid-nineteenth century, so that there are many old recipes; apple (first favourite), or blackberries, or both together.

Favourite accompaniments, besides custard or cream, were a piece of cheese (in the north), or rice pudding.

Stewed fruits

See the chapter on fruit.

Fruit fools

The fruit purée should be fairly sharp. It can be mixed with either thick cream alone, or with custard and cream. Gooseberry fool is the favourite; but see blackberry and apple fool, page 60, with the cream served separately; and rhubarb fool with dark brown sugar is excellent.

E*

Summer pudding

For a hot summer day. All kinds of soft fruits can be used.
Redcurrants and raspberries make the best one, with not too
much sugar, white bread (not sponge cake), and thick cream to
go with it (not custard). Here is a special recipe.

SUMMER PUDDING: REDCURRANTS AND RASPBERRIES

Make it the day before. Prepare the pudding basin: butter it
lightly, then line it completely with strips of white bread,
sliced fairly thin, crusts removed. Then put the redcurrants,
stringed with a fork, into a pan with the raspberries (about ½ lb
of each for a 1 to 1½-pint basin), and let them simmer with a
little sugar (no water) until hot through and the juice runs
freely. The flavour should be sharp, not too sweet. Now, put
the fruit while still hot into the basin with its bread lining.
There should be enough juice to soak well into the bread, but
the fruit should not be swimmy. Finish off with a layer of
trimmed bread as a lid. Put a saucer on top, and on top of the
saucer a weight. The weight should keep the saucer pressed
down on top of the pudding so that the juice soaks the bread
right through. Stand the basin on a stone floor, or in some cool
place, overnight.

The next day, when ready, turn out the pudding on to a
dish. Serve with a bowl of thick cream.

Baked apples

See baked apples with honey, page 128. Baked apples can be
used for a purée.

APPLE SNOW

Bake 2 apples and sieve to a purée. Add a little sugar and when cold combine with 1 or 2 beaten egg whites. Serve as soon as possible.

Apple amber

The egg yolks are used as well for an apple amber, one of the older fruit recipes. Here is one version.

AN APPLE AMBER

To a thick apple purée made with 1–2 lb cooking apples, and still hot, add demerara sugar to taste, 1–2 oz butter or margarine, lemon juice and grated lemon rind if wished, and beat well. Beat in the yolks of 2 eggs. Pour it into a buttered fire-proof dish, with room to spare for the meringue top. Whip the 2 egg whites, adding a teaspoonful of castor sugar and beating again, then fold in 3 tablespoonfuls of castor sugar. Pile the meringue mixture over the apple mixture. Sprinkle lightly with more castor sugar. Bake for just under an hour in a very slow oven (Mark 1, 275 °F). Serve hot. The meringue should be golden and crisp.

Fruit crumbles, stirabouts, cobblers

Apple crumble is very well known. Plums, prunes and/or dried apricots, rhubarb, gooseberries and other soft fruits are all good for this purpose as well.

FRUIT STIRABOUT

Make a thick batter as follows, mixed with gooseberries or chopped rhubarb or apple, or other fruit. Rub 2 oz butter or margarine into 4 oz flour, add a pinch of salt, 2–4 oz sugar, the fruit neatly prepared (about 1 lb or 1 pint), and milk to mix (about ¼ pint). Bake in a buttered pie dish for about 40 minutes in a hot oven (Mark 6, 400 °F). Serve hot, with sugar.

FRUIT COBBLER

Damsons or plums are traditional, but other fruits can be used. Cook the fruit down to a pulp with sugar. There should be about enough for a pie. Put it into a pie dish. Let it cool. Meanwhile make a rich, sweetened scone mixture: 2 oz butter or margarine rubbed into 6 oz self-raising flour, a good spoonful of sugar, and enough milk to mix to a soft dough. This is rolled out ½-inch thick and then, usually cut out as scone rounds, placed on top of the fruit. Bake in a hot oven (Mark 6, 400 °F) for about 20 minutes, until the scones are risen and golden. They can be brushed with milk first and sprinkled with sugar if wished.

Rice puddings

In the north, at any rate, a rice pudding often accompanied fruit pies and tarts, and mince pies, as well as accompanying stewed fruit. An old trick in farmhouses was to put a lump of suet in to enrich it. Sometimes nutmeg is grated on top before it goes into the oven. Long slow cooking is essential.

Pancakes

The great day for these is Shrove Tuesday, the day before the

Lent fast, sometimes called Pancake Tuesday or Pancake Day. For a batter recipe see page 99.

SHROVETIDE PANCAKES

Make the batter (page 99). Cook the pancakes so that they can be served out straight away. Heat a knob of lard in the frying-pan. When it is smoking hot, pour it off into a small warmed saucepan or heatproof jug, leaving a thin film behind in the frying-pan. Pour in enough batter just to cover the bottom of the frying-pan. Cook until brown on the underside, shaking the pan, then loosen the pancake with a palette knife, turn it over with the knife—or toss it merrily—and then let it cook on the other side. Turn it on to sugared greaseproof paper, sprinkle it with castor sugar, roll it up, and serve at once on a hot plate. Repeat the procedure, pouring in more melted lard and re-heating till smoking hot. Serve the pancakes with more sugar and wedges of lemon. Sometimes it was treacle instead.

Custards

See page 99. Remember 'a custard boiled is a custard spoiled'.

Cook a baked custard in a slow oven. A steamed custard pudding must be steamed very gently.

Junkets

See page 106.

Creams

See blackcurrant leaf cream, page 28.

Suet puddings

Gone are the days when the suet pudding, tied up like a
bolster, was boiled with the meat and the vegetables, all together in the same pot. It might be savoury or sweet, but it
was served first all the same, to take the edge off the appetite
for the meat, or the small bit of bacon. In the Victorian age
this used to be a regular cottage tea-dinner. At more pros-
perous tables the suet pudding was at that time enormously
popular: sometimes cut in slices and served with the meat
course, covered in gravy, and then again for the pudding
course, covered with treacle! But it is now in general a rarity,
and then only for cold weather, large appetites and fairly large
numbers.

The basic recipe is 8 oz flour (and perhaps a teaspoonful of
baking powder), 4 oz beef suet chopped finely (or 3 oz packet
suet), a good pinch of salt, ¼ pint water to mix.

Breadcrumbs lighten it (half fresh breadcrumbs, half flour).
An egg enriches it (with less liquid for mixing, accordingly).
Dried fruit (currants for spotted Dick) and/or moist brown
sugar, moistens and sweetens it. Milk can be used instead of
water, or, with dried fruit in the pudding, cold tea.

Mix flour, salt and suet together. Add water and mix with
the hands to a soft but firm dough. Scald and flour the pudding
cloth (unbleached calico was usual; sometimes it was an old
shirt-sleeve). To scald, dip the cloth into boiling water, wring
out. To flour, cover it well with flour on the inside. Tie the
pudding dough up in it in the shape of a rounded oblong.
Leave a little space for the pudding to swell. Tie the ends up
firmly with string.

For a jam roly-poly, roll out the paste, damp the edges,
spread with red jam, roll up, pinch the ends to seal, and tie up
in the cloth in the same way.

For a football-shaped pudding, round up the dough, put it on to the cloth, gather and tie up the ends, again leaving space for the pudding to swell.

Plunge the pudding in its cloth right into water to cover, well on the boil. An old plate on the bottom of the pan helps to prevent the pudding from catching. Cover the pan, keep on the boil, adding more boiling water if necessary, and let it boil for 2–3 hours.

These old ways are worth recording, and sometimes well worth using (a pudding boiled in a cloth is always said to be lighter); but nowadays puddings—the Christmas pudding included—are usually boiled, or more often steamed, in a basin. Follow the usual instructions, and see the notes on steamed puddings below.

For recipes for steamed suet puddings see fruit pudding below, and plum pudding, which follows it.

Steamed puddings

These may be suet, or sponge, or a light breadcrumb mixture, or custard. Note that for a pudding *boiled* in a basin, the basin is filled to the top; it must have a floured cloth tied over, with space allowed as usual for the pudding to swell, and is wholly submerged in the boiling water. For a *steamed* pudding, the basin is filled three-quarters full, buttered greaseproof paper is tied over the top (for very long steaming, as for the Christmas pudding, a scalded pudding cloth can be added, or kitchen foil); and the boiling water should come only about half way up the sides of the basin (unless a proper steamer on top of a saucepan is used).

Butter the basin well. The lid of the pan should fit well. Keep the water on the boil the whole time. Steaming takes longer than boiling.

The following is an excellent recipe for a hot fruit pudding on a cold summer's day, or at other times of the year.

FRUIT PUDDING

This is said to be glorious made with cherries in summer, but blackberries, plums or any suitable fruit can be used, or a mixture.

Make suet crust (suet paste) with 3–4 oz finely chopped suet just lightly rubbed into 8 oz flour, sifted together with 1 teaspoonful baking powder and a pinch of salt; cold water to mix. Turn it out on to a lightly floured board. Work or knead it a little and roll it out lightly, 'one way', to about ¼ inch thick. Butter your pudding basin. Now cut out the pastry to make two circles, one large for lining the basin, one smaller to cover the basin as a lid. Mould the larger circle into the basin to line it completely. Trim off with scissors, leaving a little extra over the rim. Fill the basin up with fresh fruit, 1 lb or more, ready prepared, but if cherries unstoned. Put the fruit in layer by layer, sprinkling sugar on each, with a little pinch of mixed spice if wished. Let the last layer be fruit. Add a tablespoonful of water. Damp the edges of the pastry and fit the pastry lid on the top, folding and pressing to seal. Cover with buttered greaseproof paper, tied on with string. Steam for 2–2½ hours. Serve the pudding in its basin. When serving it out, cut out the pastry lid and put it on a hot plate, and cut a slice to go with each helping of fruit.

Plum puddings

The Christmas pudding comes under this heading, but in farmhouses plum puddings were made liberally for emergencies and major occasions, especially the harvest supper. Degrees of richness varied. In the north, carrot and potato were a common ingredient, as in this typical recipe (for one pudding only). Note, it is eggless.

PLUM PUDDING (WITH CARROT AND POTATO)

4 oz flour
4 oz moist brown sugar
4 oz chopped suet
4 oz grated raw carrot
4 oz potatoes mashed with a little milk
8 oz mixed dried fruit
1 teaspoonful black treacle
½ teaspoonful mixed spice
pinch of salt

Mix dry ingredients, add the potato, kneading it in, then the treacle, lastly the carrots. Mix well. Put into a buttered basin, cover securely with buttered greaseproof paper. Steam for 4 hours. When cold and the covering dry, store for a few weeks in a cool dry place. Steam for 1½–2 hours on day of use.

Baked puddings

These are the kind of puddings most often made nowadays. Often they are baked in a pie dish. The following recipe is for a sponge pudding that can be baked in a basin.

GOLDEN PUDDING

3 tablespoonfuls golden syrup
1 tablespoonful water
4 oz butter or margarine

4 oz sugar
2 eggs
4 oz flour
pinch of salt
½ teaspoonful baking powder

Mix the syrup and water and pour into a fire-proof glass basin, well buttered. Cream margarine and sugar together. Beat the eggs in one at a time. Add the flour, salt and baking powder, sifted together. Smooth the mixture into the basin, to cover the syrup. Twist a piece of buttered greaseproof paper over the top of the basin. Bake in a moderate oven (Mark 4, 350 °F) for ¾ hour. Turn the pudding out on to a hot dish.

Hurry puddings

Hurry sounds better than hasty. The 'hasty puddings' of the past were usually dollops of batter dropped into boiling water, and have an aura of washing day. 'Hurry' covers all the quick recipes. Most of us like to collect them, but beware of quick rubbery sponges. Castle puddings are better and can be made in ramekin dishes or patty tins instead of the traditional little tin moulds; see cake puddings below for a variation on the same theme. Bread fritters are useful, on the lines of *pain perdu*; or thin jam sandwiches, crusts removed, can be fried in butter.

BREAD FRITTERS

Beat up an egg together with a dessertspoonful of sugar and ½ cup of milk. Cut 4 slices of bread into strips or halves, dip them into the egg mixture, and fry in a little butter. Serve hot, sprinkled with sugar.

Double-purpose puddings

These are the puddings that can also be used as cakes. Cheese cakes (page 119) come into this category, and 'tartlets', and apple cakes (page 157). Hot gingerbread sponge, cut in squares, served with custard or cream makes a favourite pudding course, and the remainder can go towards tea-time. The cake puddings below can be served hot with jam sauce, or as little cakes cold or warm; they can be warmed up in the oven.

CAKE PUDDINGS

Take the weight of 2 eggs in flour (self-raising), sugar and butter. Half melt the butter, beat it to a cream, then add the eggs well beaten, then the sugar, then the flour with grated lemon peel. Bake $\frac{1}{2}$ hour in little cups (about 20 minutes in patty tins), in a moderately hot oven (Mark 5, 375 °F). Serve with a sauce.

12. Country Baking

HOME-MADE BREAD

The history of baking differs according to regions and includes the use of the bakestone, the girdle (or griddle), and ovens of various kinds, shapes and sizes. In remote country places especially, the baking of bread for the family was a continual responsibility and could be a great labour, with all kinds of problems involved. Even in the early years of this century a country cottager's wife might still have to use a brick oven and faggots to heat it, yeast saved from home brewing, and perhaps as much as a bushel (4 stone) of flour a week, ground at the nearest mill, if her household was large and bread much the largest part of the diet. Often the slices had to be carefully counted out and shared round.

Weights and measures

Old recipe quantities are based on a stone of flour (14 lb). A batch of bread might be made from the whole of this amount, mixed in a great big pancheon (mixing bowl), to make about 12 large loaves; or from a gallon of flour: ½ stone (7 lb); or from ¼ stone (hence the 3½-lb bag of flour). More recent recipes are based on the 3-lb bag of flour (for 2 large or 4 small loaves), now replaced by the metric bag (1·5 kg), which works out at rather more (nearly 5 oz) than 3 lb and a little less than 3½ lb.

Pots and tins

As a guide, two or three 2-lb tins or four 1-lb tins for about 3 lb flour, but bread can be baked in cake tins, earthenware garden flower pots (5-inch size is usual), fairly shallow round earthenware pans (earthenware 'bread-bakers' are sometimes available), or on a greased or floured baking-sheet. Earthenware should be well but lightly greased. Flower pots and bread-bakers should be baked empty, well greased, for 30 minutes or so, at least three times, before they are used for bread-making. Tins are usually greased, sometimes floured, sometimes both greased and floured for a crisp crust. Fill tins or pots about half full with the dough, which should rise almost to the top before being put into the oven.

Ingredients for bread-making

Flour. The subject is highly complicated, but the following are simplified notes on the usual flours for home baking nowadays.

For bread use plain flour not self-raising. 'Strong' plain white bread flour is now mainly used. Its high gluten content (see below) makes the dough springier. 'Soft' white flour (the ordinary 'household' flour, for cakes and general purposes) gives flatter results.

Note: Flour consists mainly of gluten (vegetable protein; heat makes it elastic, then firms it) and starch. Wheat grown in the British Isles is low in gluten and is therefore described as 'weak' or 'soft' wheat. Imported North American 'hard' wheat is used for milling the 'strong' flours.

Wholemeal flour is used for brown bread and is more nutritious than white flour. Flours described as 100 per cent wholemeal (wholewheat or whole wheatmeal) have the whole grain of the wheat, 'nothing extracted or added', and so contain

the valuable wheatgerm and the roughage supplied by the
husk and bran; the bread tends to be heavy. Flours described
as wheatmeal have the husk and bran partially removed, giving
a (usually specified) lower percentage of whole grain. Either
type can be mixed at home with either 'strong' or 'soft' white
flour, in proportions according to preference, to lighten the
bread.

Wholemeal and wheatmeal flours are unbleached. The flour
may be milled from 'compost grown' wheat (organically
grown, without the use of chemical fertilizers), but it may contain a proportion of imported 'hard' wheat (not organically
grown) to strengthen the gluten content. In the old traditional
way it should be stone ground (as opposed to roller-milled), in
this way retaining the wheatgerm. The description on the
flour bag should give the relevant information.

White flour is usually chemically bleached, but some 'strong'
white flours are unbleached, and then the colour is creamy and
the bread will probably taste more like bread. Ordinary 'household' flour is nearly always ultra refined and chemically treated.

Yeast. In the past brewer's yeast (liquid, bitter, referred to as
'barm' in old recipes) was used for raising the bread. Baker's
yeast (compressed, putty-like, at first known as German yeast)
is used nowadays. Fresh yeast should be bought from a fresh
supply, and kept cool and dry and used soon. It can be stored
for a few days in an airtight container in the refrigerator. Dried
yeast (granules, for reconstituting, stronger than fresh yeast) is
more widely available and a useful alternative. It can be kept
for a few months in an airtight tin. As a rule, use half as much
dried yeast when substituting for fresh yeast. For traditional
methods the customary allowance is $\frac{1}{2}$ oz fresh yeast for up to
$1\frac{1}{2}$ lb flour, then 1 oz for up to $3\frac{1}{2}$ lb, $1\frac{1}{2}$–2 oz for 7 lb. A little
more yeast is usual for wholemeal flour.

Note: Yeast is a plant. It consists of living cells. To multiply, it needs warmth, food and moisture. As it multiplies, gas (carbon dioxide) is formed, which raises the dough. Gentle heat activates it. Cold arrests it. Too much heat kills it, as does the heat of the oven when the bread is baked, but the yeast has then done its work.

Salt. Slows down fermentation, improves texture and flavour. 1 teaspoonful salt to 1 lb flour is a usual allowance, but to give the bread more flavour more salt is often preferred.

Sugar. Aids fermentation and in the ordinary way just a little is creamed with the yeast (see basic recipe below), but not always.

Water. About ½ pint to 1 lb flour, but the amount depends on the absorbency of the flour. It must not be too hot, or it will kill the yeast. Tepid, about ⅔ cold water and ⅓ boiling water, is right.

Milk. Sweetens, helps bread keep, and is sometimes substituted for some of the water. In the past skimmed milk was much used for bread-making. A little milk can be brushed over the top of the loaf for a 'gilded' effect, if this is liked.

Fat. Up to 1 oz, sometimes more, butter, lard or margarine to 1 lb flour is sometimes rubbed into the flour, or melted in with the liquid, to help the bread keep longer. The crust will be softer.

Basic recipe

Bread recipes differ in all sorts of ways. Some people rest content with the first recipe that they try; others cast around until they find one that suits them and their domestic life. Perhaps an extra quick method, or an extra slow one which might involve mixing the dough last thing at night and leaving it in a cold place to be proved and baked the next day. The following recipe, for small quantities, gives the step by step details for making ordinary household bread using simple traditional methods, and can act as a basis for comparing other recipes, old or new.

Note: 'a warm place' in bread recipes used to mean the hearth by the kitchen fire, or a rack over it. It can be over a cooker, near a boiler, perhaps in an airing cupboard, anywhere suitable where the dough can keep warm but not get hot.

Note also that 'proving' and 'rising' mean much the same and are used almost interchangeably. Rising proves that the yeast is working.

STEP BY STEP LOAF

1 large or 2 small loaves

> 1½ lb strong plain white bread flour
> 1½ teaspoonfuls salt
> ½ oz fresh yeast (or 2 teaspoonfuls dried yeast)
> 1 teaspoonful sugar
> ¾ pint tepid water
> 1 oz melted lard (optional)

1. *Put out everything needed*. Boil a kettle and have the room warm and not draughty.

2. *Measure the flour* (in breakfast cups). Put it in a large mixing bowl with the chill off (6-pint size will do), sprinkle it round the edge with the salt and leave it in a warm place. Have a little extra flour in reserve.

3. *Cream the yeast*. Crumble it into a small basin and mix to a

cream with the sugar and about a third of the tepid water. If using dried yeast, follow the instructions supplied. Leave it in a warm place until frothy (about 10 minutes). It should smell sweet and fresh.

Note: The creamed yeast with about half or more of the water is sometimes put into a well in the centre of the warmed flour, with a little flour sprinkled over, and left in the warm for 20 minutes or so, until the surface is covered with bubbles. This is known as 'sponging' or 'setting the sponge' and is meant to improve the texture, but is usually now omitted.

4. *Mix the dough.* Stir the creamed yeast with a fork and pour it all into a well in the flour. Add nearly all the rest of the water. Have a little extra water in reserve. Add melted lard if used. Then plunge warmed hands in and mix. If too dry, add smallest amount more of tepid water. If too wet and sticky, add smallest sprinkling of flour.

Start to knead as soon as the dough comes away from the sides of the bowl. The dough should be springy. Double it up, fold it over, knuckle it down. Continue to knead in this way, quite lightly but thoroughly, for 5–10 minutes, until hands and bowl are quite clean and the dough like a cushion. Slap it aside, flour it lightly, and slap it back.

5. *Leave the dough to rise.* Cover the top of the bowl with a tea towel and a thick cloth and leave it in a warm place. Do something else for an hour or so until the dough has doubled its size. Test with a finger for lightness.

6. *Prepare the tins* in the meantime. Grease two 1-lb (about 1½-pint capacity) bread tins, or one 2-lb tin, and put in a warm place.

7. *Knead again.* Punch the risen dough down and knead it hard for about 5 minutes, either still in the bowl or on a

floured wooden board. It should be supple and smooth. Cut it into 2 equal pieces, if making 2 loaves, knead them roughly to size and put into the tins. The tins should be half full.

8. *Leave to rise again*. This stage is often called 'proving'. Cover the tins with a tea towel and stand them in the warm for the dough to 'rest and recover'. It should double in size again. Allow about 20–30 minutes.

Put the mixing bowl to soak in cold water.

See in good time to the oven. It should be hot (Mark 7, 425 °F) ready for baking.

9. *Bake the bread*. The dough should have risen nearly to the tops of the tins. Put the tins into the preheated oven (Mark 7, 425 °F), centre shelf, and bake for 35 minutes or longer, reducing the heat a little, to moderately hot (Mark 5, 375 °F), after the first 15 minutes.

10. *Test the loaves*. Don't look in the oven too soon. Test by tapping the top crust. If it feels firm and crisp turn the loaf out of the tin. Tap the bottom crust. If it sounds hollow, the loaf is done. If it seems not quite ready, put it back in the oven, bottom side up in the tin, for a little bit longer.

11. *Stand the loaves to cool*. Put them on a wire rack, or leaning against a wooden board, or stand them on end on the dresser.

To store bread

Store the bread when quite cold. It must have some air or it will soon go musty or mouldy. Avoid tins or plastic containers. An enamel bread bin (with an air hole in the lid) can be fairly satisfactory. Wipe it out frequently. An old-fashioned stoneware or earthenware bread crock (or bread mug) is usually better. Sometimes it has a lid, but the top can quite well be covered with a bread board or a clean cloth. Alternatively, wrap the bread in a tea towel or stand it on a wooden board or shelf, covered with a tea towel or muslin.

To reheat bread

Give it 5–10 minutes in a moderate or very moderate oven. It can be covered with a tin or wrapped in greaseproof paper if wished, to prevent it from hardening.

To cut fresh bread

Use a hot knife.

Toast

Bread about two days old toasts well. For crisp toast bang the piece of toast with a wooden spoon as soon as done. This drives off the steam. Serve straight away in a toast rack, or leaning up against anything suitable, or in a folded napkin— not a paper one or the toast will go leathery. For hot buttered toast cut the bread not too thin, butter the toast immediately, serve at once piled on a hot dish, or keep it covered for just a few minutes in a warm place.

Sometimes it is more than tempting to collect quotations as well as recipes. Toast seems a special subject for eloquence, especially in *The Wind in the Willows*—the plate of hot buttered toast that the warder's daughter brings Toad. In *Lark Rise to Candleford* the description of how the hamlet people gave hospitality to their visitors continues: 'In winter, salt butter would be sent for [from the shop at the inn] and toast would be made and eaten with celery. Toast was a favourite dish for family consumption. "I've made 'em a stack o' toast as high as up to their knees", a mother would say on a winter Sunday afternoon before her hungry brood came in from church. Another dish upon which they prided themselves was thin slices of cold, boiled streaky bacon on toast, a dish so delicious that it deserves to be more widely popular.'

Yeast mixtures

Recipes for traditional yeast mixtures are widespread. Good ones to collect include recipes for hot cross buns (for Good Friday), fruit breads (sometimes called plum bread or spice bread), tea cakes (to eat plain or toasted), and dough cakes (often made from spare bread dough, with lard, sugar and dried fruit added, and sometimes spice).

SPICED FRUIT LOAF

8 oz strong plain white bread flour
large pinch of salt
2 teaspoonfuls dried yeast
¼ pint tepid milk
1 oz soft brown sugar
½ teaspoonful mixed spice
1 oz butter or margarine
4 oz dried fruit (currants and sultanas, mixed)
castor sugar and boiling water, to glaze

Have everything warm. Put the flour in the mixing bowl in a warm place. Cream the yeast in a mug or small basin with one third of the tepid milk and 1 teaspoonful of the sugar: whisk with a fork and leave, covered with a piece of paper, in a warm place for 10-15 minutes, to froth up. Mix the spice with the rest of the sugar. Soften the butter and melt it in the rest of the milk. Mix butter and milk, tepid not hot, with the yeast, adding the sugar and spice. Make a well in the flour, sprinkle salt round the edge, and pour the yeast mixture in. Mix and beat for 5 minutes with a wooden spoon, adding a drop more milk if necessary, to make a fairly loose dough. Then beat in the dried fruit, distributing it evenly throughout. Turn the dough straight into a round 7-inch cake tin which has been warmed and well buttered. Cover with a tea towel. Leave in a fairly warm place to rise until doubled in size, about 1–1½ hours. The oven should be ready and hot (Mark 6, 400 °F). Bake the loaf for ¾–1 hour, reducing the heat to Mark 5, 375 °F after the first 10 minutes. Test with a knitting needle. Rap the base of the loaf when removed from the tin, to make sure it is cooked through. Dissolve 1 teaspoonful of castor sugar in 2 teaspoonfuls of boiling water and brush the top with this glaze while the loaf is still hot. Leave to cool on a wire rack. Cut when cold, slicing it crossways. It can be eaten plain, when fresh, or with butter. When kept, it toasts well.

Soda bread

In places where yeast was hard to obtain, and especially in Ireland, then soda bread was the answer. Its fame has spread. It is very quick and easy to make, and most people like it. In the old way in Ireland it went into the pot oven (sometimes known as a bastable oven), the all-purpose three-legged iron pot with a lid, glowing turf placed on top to give an even heat. Soda bread is made traditionally with wholemeal flour, bread soda (bicarbonate of soda), and buttermilk or slightly sour milk. Fresh milk, or fresh milk and warm water mixed, can be used instead, with cream of tartar added for acidity, as in the following recipe.

F

WHOLEMEAL SODA BREAD

1 lb wholemeal (whole wheatmeal) flour
1 teaspoonful salt
1 teaspoonful bicarbonate of soda
1 teaspoonful cream of tartar
milk and warm water to mix (about 6 fluid oz
  of each)

Run the flour, salt and raising agents together with the finger-tips in a warmed bowl. Stir milk and warm water together. Add it nearly all at once, then a little more if necessary, mixing with the blade of a knife to a moist dough that will turn clean out of the bowl. Do not knead, but dust with flour and turn it out as a flattish round, patting lightly to shape, on a greased or floured baking sheet. In the usual way, if wished, cut a large deepish cross on the top with a floured knife. Bake at once in a moderately hot oven (Mark 5, 375 °F) for about 40 minutes. Tap the base. It should sound hollow when done. A knitting-needle should come out clean. Cool on a wire rack. For a soft crust wrap in a tea towel. Cut when cold.

Scones and tea breads

Recipes for scones and also for tea breads made without yeast are very widely available and usually very straightforward and easy to follow. For scones, as for soda bread, always work quickly, add all or nearly all the liquid at once, mix it in with the blade of a knife, handle the dough very lightly, bake straight away. For oatmeal scones see page 122.

COUNTRY CAKES

Cakes were firstly for special occasions: for christenings, birthdays and weddings, funeral cakes, simnel cakes for Mothering Sunday in the middle of Lent (though they are now more often for Easter), the Christmas cake, and cakes for the harvest. Then, in the nineteenth century, with easier methods, cheaper ingredients, and the rising importance of sweet things for 'tea', home baking began really to flourish; cakes were made in great quantity and variety, and as a sign of good housekeeping. Then, thirdly, bought cakes largely took over.

Straightforward cakes that keep well have a special place in the country tradition, and some of the recipes can be particularly useful today: for packed lunches, or instead of a pudding, and in addition to the bread and butter, scones, oatcakes, savoury sandwiches, buttered or dripping toast, potted meats, lettuces, watercress, that are the tea-time alternatives to too many sweet things in the diet.

All the following groups include recipes that are well worth collecting.

Rich fruit cakes

A good rich one for Christmas, perhaps not quite such a rich one for birthdays, and they can also be very useful for picnics and summer holidays. Note that rich fruit cakes are usually best made 3 or 4 weeks in advance, and then stored in an airtight tin to mature.

Plain fruit cakes

Usually the rub in, not the creaming method, and they can be made with lard and butter or margarine mixed, or with clarified dripping (page 113). Sometimes eggless. Sometimes sugarless, relying on the dried fruit for sweetness. They include soda cakes, lunch cakes, and the economical big farmhouse currant cakes.

FARMHOUSE CURRANT CAKE

14 oz self-raising flour
6 oz lard and butter mixed
4 oz sugar
10 oz currants
milk to mix

Rub the fat into the flour. Add the sugar and currants, and milk to mix (¼ pint or a little more). Bake in a well-greased deep cake tin (8-inch diameter) in a moderate oven (Mark 4, 350 °F) for about an hour.

Gingerbreads and parkins

Again economical. Gingerbreads, and parkins (page 122), keep well and are very popular, and useful for many occasions. They burn easily and need a slow or moderate oven.

HALF AND HALF GINGERBREAD

2 oz lard
2 oz margarine
4 oz golden syrup
4 oz black treacle
6 oz wholewheat flour
6 oz plain white flour
3 oz soft brown sugar
pinch of salt

2 teaspoonfuls ground ginger
1 teaspoonful bicarbonate of soda
milk to mix (about ¼ pint)

Melt the lard and margarine in a saucepan, with the syrup and treacle, then add to the flour, sugar, salt and ginger mixed together. Add the bicarbonate of soda, dissolved in a little milk, and mix with a little more milk to make a soft mixture. Grease a meat tin, about 10 by 8 inches, and line it with a sheet of greased greaseproof paper. Smooth the mixture into it. Bake in a very moderate oven (Mark 3, 325 °F) for about 45 minutes, until a knitting needle comes out clean. Let it cool in the tin. When it is cold put it into an airtight tin. Preferably keep for a day or two before cutting.

Apple cakes

A special feature of country cookery. They vary widely. Some are made with pastry, coming under the heading of a tart or a pasty. One such apple cake, baked as a rectangular pasty, has a filling of thinly sliced apple with a little sugar, and on top of this, before the covering of pastry is added, a sprinkling of grated cheese. Some are made with a cake batter. Some are spiced and some not. Some include eggs and some don't. Sometimes stewed apples are used, but most of them are made with raw apple, sometimes sliced, sometimes chopped. Most of them can be used either as a tea-time cake or as a pudding (see double-purpose puddings, page 143).

DORSET APPLE CAKE

4 oz butter or margarine
8 oz self-raising flour

    4 oz granulated sugar
    8 oz chopped apple
    milk to mix

Rub the fat into the flour as for pastry, add the sugar, then the apple (peeled, cored and roughly chopped: about 1½ breakfast cups). Mix well, adding a little milk, to make a stiff dough. Put the mixture into a meat tin about 10 by 8 inches, greased and lined with greased paper. Bake in a moderately hot oven (Mark 5, 375 °F), for about 40 minutes.

    Eat hot with sugar, hot or cold with custard or cream, or warm, split and buttered.

Small cakes and sandwich cakes

'The weight of an egg' (page 100) is the classic mixture. Use 2 eggs for a 7-inch sandwich cake; with eggs of an average size the quantities work out as follows.

VICTORIA SANDWICH

    2 eggs
    4 oz butter or margarine (or 2 oz of each)
    4 oz castor sugar
    4 oz self-raising flour

Cream butter and sugar together. Beat the eggs in one by one, adding a little flour. Fold in the rest of the flour, adding a tablespoonful of warm water and mixing well. Put the mixture into two buttered 7-inch sandwich tins and bake until golden in a moderately hot oven (Mark 5, 375 °F), 15–20 minutes. Turn out upside down on to a wire cake rack. To fill, spread one half with the filling and put the other, baked side upwards, on top.

The mixture can be flavoured by using vanilla sugar, or rosemary sugar (page 22), or with a little cinnamon, or grated orange or lemon rind, and see page 32 for use of scented-geranium leaves. The filling can be jam, or a butter cream, lemon curd, a fruit butter (page 165), or fruit and thick cream. Fill with jam while the cake is still warm; for the other fillings wait until it has cooled. The top can be iced, or dusted with castor or icing sugar.

Alternatively, the above quantities make about 18 small cakes in bun tins or patty tins. Bake for about 12 minutes.

No tin is needed for rock cakes. I have always called them rock buns.

ROCK BUNS

8 oz flour
1 teaspoonful baking-powder
pinch of salt
¼ teaspoonful ground nutmeg
1½ oz margarine
1½ oz lard
3 oz sugar (soft pale brown or castor)
3 oz currants
1 oz candied peel (optional)
1 egg
milk to mix

Sift flour, salt, baking-powder and nutmeg all together. Cut and rub in the lard and margarine. Add sugar and dried fruit, then beat up the egg with a little milk (about 4 tablespoonfuls) and mix it in with a fork to make a stiff mixture. Put it out, with spoon and fork or two forks, in rough heaps on to a well-greased baking-sheet. Bake in a hot oven (Mark 6, 400 °F) for ¼ hour. Makes a dozen.

Biscuits and shortbread

Small biscuits are mostly too fiddly and time-consuming to be made now at home very often. Home-made shortbread is still a great standby. It keeps excellently, in a tin, and goes well with coffee, and also fruit fools and stewed fruit. It must be made with butter. Two-four-six is a good formula.

SHORTBREAD (TWO-FOUR-SIX)

    2 oz castor sugar
    4 oz butter
    6 oz flour

Sift the sugar and flour together, adding a small pinch of salt. Beat the butter in a warmed bowl, using a wooden spoon, until very soft, then work in the other ingredients with the hand until lightly bound. Smooth the mixture into an ungreased 7-inch sandwich tin with a loose base. Prick lightly over the top with a fork. Bake in a very moderate oven (Mark 3, 325 °F) for about 40 minutes, until a very pale brown. Cut into wedges or shapes in the tin while still warm. Cool on a wire rack. Store, when cold, in an airtight tin.

The traditional Easter biscuits are among the best biscuit recipes. They have their slight variations. In the West Country they were coloured golden with saffron.

EASTER BISCUITS

    8 oz flour
    ¼ teaspoonful mixed spice
    ¼ teaspoonful cinnamon
    4 oz butter (or margarine)

4 oz castor sugar
2 oz currants
lemon juice
1 egg
1 tablespoonful brandy (optional)

Sift the flour and spices together. Rub in the butter. Add sugar and currants, and just a little lemon juice. Beat the egg, with the brandy as well if included, then mix all to a paste. Put it on to a floured board. Knead lightly, roll out ¼-inch thick. Cut out with a fluted biscuit-cutter of the usual size (about 2½-inch); or the size of a small saucer (5-inch) is still sometimes the custom. Bake on greased baking trays in a moderate oven (Mark 4, 350 °F), about ¼ hour. They must not brown up.

They were sometimes called Easter cakes.

13. Jams and Jellies

Preserving preserves happy days: the memory of a particular garden or hedgerow, wherever the fruit was gathered, at a particular time of the year. The dates on the labels act as a diary.

As most country jam recipes take a knowledge of the main rules for granted, it is useful to have them collected together for reference.

Rules for jam-making

Fruit. It should be dry, firm, just ripe, sound and fresh. If fruit is wet or overripe, the jam might go mouldy when stored. Pick over and wash the fruit just before using.

Utensils. Use very clean scalded utensils. Small quantities of jam can be made in a suitable large heavy saucepan instead of in a preserving-pan, but the pan *must* be large enough or the jam will boil over. Use a wooden spoon. Use clean, dry, warm jam jars. To heat and sterilize, bake them in a very slow oven (Mark ½, 250 °F) for ¼ hour.

Sugar. Granulated sugar is commonly used. Ordinary lump sugar is good. Special preserving sugar is excellent for a good bright colour, and less stirring and skimming is needed; it is often used for show jams and jellies. Brown sugars can be used, but burn more easily and will alter colour and flavour. They make a good dark breakfast marmalade. For the use of honey see page 128.

Quantities. As a rule, 5 lb of jam should be obtained from 3 lb of sugar. 1 lb sugar to 1 lb fruit is the usual allowance, but ¾ lb sugar to each 1 lb fruit often works out very well. The most sugar is allowed for sharp fruits such as gooseberries that are rich in pectin (up to 1¼ lb sugar to 1 lb fruit). Tables indicating the quality of pectin and acid content are helpful, but much depends on the variety of a particular fruit, degree of ripeness and the weather conditions of a particular season. Too little sugar results in a jam that may not set well or keep well, and too much spoils the flavour and is likely to crystallize. Without experience, it is best to keep to a recipe.

Procedure. (a) Cook the fruit without sugar initially, with or without water according to type of fruit and the recipe. Cook slowly. This is to soften the fruit and extract the pectin, the sticky substance which gives a good set. Acid assists the process, and is added, usually in the form of lemon juice, to fruits deficient in acid, especially cherries and strawberries; unless they are combined with an acid fruit or its juice, such as currants or gooseberries—both of which are rich in pectin as well.

(b) Add the sugar. If warmed first it dissolves quicker. Stir, and do not let the juice boil, until the sugar is fully dissolved.

(c) Boil rapidly. Stir now and again, to prevent sticking and burning.

(d) Test for setting. Usually after 10 minutes, or according to recipe. The usual way is the saucer test: put a little of the jam on a cold saucer, let it cool slightly, and then the setting-point is reached if the jam wrinkles when pushed with the finger-tip or a spoon. Remove pan from the heat meanwhile.

Skimming. Remove scum, if necessary, at the last. Either skim with a metal spoon, or add a scrap of butter and stir, with the pan off the heat.

To pot and cover. Follow any special directions. In the ordinary way pour the hot jam into hot jars (if they are cold they will crack). A scalded heat-proof jug can be helpful. Fill jars very full. Wipe clean. Add waxed discs, placed on the jam waxed side down, straight away. Add cellophane covers, moistened on the side away from the jam and secured with a rubber band, when the jam has cooled. Packets of jam-pot covers, containing waxed discs, cellophane covers, rubber bands and small labels, can be bought from most stationers.

Label with name and date and store in a cool, dark, dry, fairly well-ventilated place. Too much warmth may make the jam shrink.

BLACKCURRANT JAM

Plenty of sugar can be used for blackcurrants. They must be simmered very gently indeed, probably for at least ½ hour, before the sugar is added, or the skins will be tough.

> 2 lb blackcurrants
> 3 lb sugar
> 1 pint water

Stalk and wash the fruit. Put it into the preserving pan, add cold water (1 pint or a little over), bring slowly up to the boil, and simmer very gently indeed, stirring gently and shaking the pan, until the skins are soft. Remove from the heat, add the warmed sugar, stir until the sugar is well dissolved. Then boil, not too fast, stirring meanwhile, until setting-point (about 5 minutes, or longer). Pour into warmed jars and cover.

Blackcurrant jam keeps well. For its use for colds see page 172.

Mixed fruit jams

Useful for small amounts of different kinds of fruit. Plum and apple, equal weights, was a very popular mixture, sometimes with an equal weight of pears as well. 1 lb sugar to each 1 lb of mixed fruit is the usual allowance. Experiments usually work out successfully.

Quick methods for raspberries or blackberries

Again useful for small amounts. Examples are worth collecting, such as the following. These preserves usually keep very well and have a very good flavour.

QUICK PRESERVE

Equal weights of blackberries, or raspberries, and sugar. Put the fruit into the pan. Add the sugar, warmed through first in the oven so that it quickly dissolves. Bring up to the boil. Let it boil quite fast for 3 minutes. Pot and cover.

Fruit butters

These were made as a variation. As in the case of fruit cheeses, the name relates to the consistency. Fruit butters are simply a spread made from fruit well cooked down in a little cider (for apples) or water, with spice to flavour (cinnamon, cloves or mixed spice)—until smooth and creamy; then sugar, stirred in over a low heat until dissolved, is added to taste: not as much as for jam, and consequently this preserve does not keep very long, and is not often worth making nowadays, though it can be quite useful as an emergency jam or for filling a sandwich cake.

Fruit cheeses

These need plenty of fruit to boil down to a pulp and then sieve; and then *long* slow cooking after sugar is added as for jam (usually 1 lb sugar to each 1 lb of the purée)—and careful stirring, until the paste comes clean away from the side of the pan. They should be much stiffer than jam. They keep excellently. They are potted in small pots or jars, in the same way as for jam, and can be turned out and cut into slices, like cheese. These fruit cheeses were a very popular old preserve, and were sometimes set in special moulds with a pattern. Damson cheese is still a great favourite.

Jellies

Sharp fruits are best. The fruit is cooked initially (see procedure for jam-making, page 163), usually with ¼ to 1 pint of water to each 1 lb of fruit, but depending on the fruit and the recipe. After that, the juice is strained overnight through a jelly bag or a cloth—or sometimes it is just put through a nylon strainer quite quickly, though the jelly will not be so clear. The strained juice is then measured, and put into the pan and heated; sugar is added (usually 1 lb sugar to each 1 pint of the juice); and when the sugar is well dissolved, the juice is boiled as quickly as possible until it jells. Test for setting-point as for jam (page 163). It should jell just lightly. Pot in small jars, add waxed discs and cover (page 164). Don't move the jars until the jelly has set.

To set up a jelly bag: This was sometimes made of flannel, for very clear jellies, which was troublesome to 'keep in order'. Unbleached calico, strong cheesecloth, a few thicknesses of butter muslin, or an old white cotton pillowcase—any clean, fresh, scalded cloth that will take the weight of the fruit and strain the juice gently will do. It can be slung up on two kitchen chairs, if the chair legs have cross-bars. Turn one chair upside down on to the seat of another. Tie the corners or loops of the jelly cloth, round the cross-bars, to the four up-turned chair legs. Stand a large basin on the upside-down chair seat below. Alternatively, the cloth can be tied up with string and hung from a hook or a rack.

Favourite jellies for tea-time are blackberry jelly (very good with hot scones), crab apple jelly (ideal with thin brown bread and butter), quince jelly (remarkable flavour and a beautiful colour).

For jellies to accompany meat see page 90.

APPLE JELLY

Can be made from windfalls, chopped up, skin, cores and all, with all damaged pieces cut out, and cooked in water to cover, until very soft. Then proceed as above, adding 1 lb sugar to each 1 pint of the juice after it has been measured and heated. The apples while cooking can be flavoured with a few sprigs of fresh mint (then the jelly can be used with roast lamb); or some bruised root ginger, a small amount; or 1 or 2 cloves, or a few scented-geranium leaves (page 31). Or the measured juice while boiling can be flavoured with a little strained lemon or orange juice and thinly pared rind tied in muslin; or with cloves or bruised ginger to taste, tied in muslin.

Hedgerow and wild-fruit jams and jellies

For a list of fruits see page 59. Most of these fruits can be dusty and need careful washing. The small berries have to be gathered in quantities to make even a small amount of jelly or jam. They are often combined with apple. The following recipes contain a larger proportion of apple than usual.

APPLE AND ELDERBERRY JAM

1 lb cooking apples
¼ lb elderberries
½ pint water
¾ lb sugar

A small amount, to try out. Peel, core and chop apples, wash the elderberries and strip from their sprays. Put the apples into the pan with ½ pint of cold water and stew them until cooked down. Add elderberries and cook, stirring, for 5 minutes longer. Withdraw from heat, add warmed sugar, stir till dissolved. Bring slowly up to the boil, then boil quite rapidly till setting-point. The colour will turn rich and dark. Clear the scum. Pour into small heated jars, add waxed discs, then add covers.

SLOE AND APPLE JELLY JAM

¾ lb ripe sloes
1½ lb cooking apples
water
1 lb sugar to each 1 pint pulp

Simmer the sloes with the chopped up apples, unpeeled and uncored, in just enough water to cover, until cooked down to a pulp. Strain through a nylon strainer or sieve. Add 1 lb sugar to 1 pint pulp, stir until sugar dissolved, then boil until setting-point. Pot and cover.

14. Drinks and Remedies

Beer was the main country household drink in most regions, until tea drinking took hold during the second half of the eighteenth century. In some of the farms and cottages the old ways of home brewing continued into this present century, although in general the custom had largely died out. Sometimes herb beers were made, from wild herbs such as yarrow or nettles. Home-made wines, from plants of the field and hedgerow and garden, were for special occasions and for a glass to keep out the cold. Today there is a revival of interest in home brewing and wine-making; and also in the very old country use of herb teas, which, unless described as tisanes and regarded as continental, have for some time been almost forgotten.

Herb teas

The general rules are as follows, but they may be varied somewhat in the case of a particular herb or recipe.

Never use a metal teapot or strainer, or it will spoil the flavour. Use fresh herbs, or dried herbs of a good flavour and colour. Unless a recipe indicates otherwise, use 3 teaspoonfuls of fresh herbs for each cup; or, because the flavour is concentrated, 1 teaspoonful of dried herbs. Bruise fresh herbs to bring out the flavour. Warm the teapot, put the herbs in the pot, pour boiling water over, leave to infuse for 5–10 minutes, strain into a cup or glass, and drink. A tea for one person can be made in an earthenware mug with a saucer over the top, instead of using a teapot. Strain it off when it is ready. The best sweetener is honey.

Lemon balm tea has a delicate flavour and is beneficial at all hours; lime flower tea and elderflower tea are fragrant, soothing, and good for colds, also helpful towards a good night's sleep; mint tea is a clear green and refreshing; peppermint tea is highly regarded and was sometimes served in small wine-glasses on formal occasions; parsley tea (a good handful of parsley) is highly thought of for rheumatism (an old gardeners' remedy); sage tea was widely drunk as a tonic, and used as a cold cure (some mint can go with it, and it can be sweetened with honey); woodruff tea (dried leaves are better) tastes of new mown hay, though some say dried grass, and is both reviving and soothing (it needs about 15 minutes to infuse, and hot but not boiling water should be used for this tea); chamomile tea, to ward off colds, aches and pains, is what Peter Rabbit was given after escaping from Mr. MacGregor's garden.

Thirst-quenchers

Shepherds' and harvest drinks were more than thirst-quenchers merely. They were often made with oatmeal or barley, to be strengthening as well as refreshing, though by modern standards the old recipes can taste rather anaemic. Lemon barley water was often made at home for invalids; there are various methods. Drinks of this kind for invalids and 'those in health' were usually made quite mild in flavour.

LEMON BARLEY WATER

1 oz pearl barley (2 tablespoonfuls)
rind of 1 lemon
1 pint boiling water

Wash the barley, using a strainer. Put it into a heat-proof jug. Wash the lemon well. Peel the rind very thin and put it with the barley, then pour the boiling water into the jug. Cover, and let it stand overnight. Strain it next day. Add a little sugar if wished.

Note: Only the yellow rind should be peeled off the lemon; not the white pith, which is bitter.

APPLE WATER

1 or 2 sharp apples
¾ pint boiling water
sugar to taste

Wash the apple(s). Do not peel, but slice thinly. Put the slices into a heat-proof jug and pour on to them boiling water. Add a little sugar if wished. Stir round. Cover. Strain when cool. Sometimes just apple peel is used.

RHUBARB WATER

1 or 2 sticks of young rhubarb
1 or 2 rounded tablespoonfuls sugar
1 pint boiling water

Wipe and trim the rhubarb, but do not peel. Slice thin. Make the drink as for apple water above.

Cold cures

These might be for an actual cold or cough, or for when somebody came in from the cold. They included all kinds of possets, syrups and cordials—elderberry and blackcurrant were favourites. Onion, as gruel or soup, or mashed up with butter, and sometimes for a bad cold sniffed raw, was highly regarded. Sometimes the remedy was a herb tea: sage tea (see above), or young raspberry leaf tea. Sometimes a spoonful of black treacle dissolved in hot milk, or of blackcurrant jam in hot water. Honey and lemon is still very popular.

HONEY AND LEMON

A spoonful of honey, the juice of a lemon, a little hot water, and it can be stiffened with whisky.

For children, orange and lemon juice mixed is often liked very much.

Honey

(See also Chapter 10, page 126.) It goes particularly well with herb teas and is soothing for colds and coughs, as mentioned above. Stirred into any warm drink that is suitable, it makes a good nightcap. It is also very reviving.

'INSTANT REVIVER'

Stir 1 or 2 teaspoonfuls of honey into a cup of hot coffee, with milk or without.

Index